MAGIC in a BOTTLE

The Untold Story of
Arnie Esterer
and
Markko Vineyard

eb & Dom
With the Very best wishes
Cheers
Arnie

4/13/19
Thank you so much.
Cheers.

CLIFFORD G. ANNIS, JR.

outskirts press

The book is dedicated first to my late father, Clifford Sr. and mother, Nancy, who taught me to never settle for second best, set a goal and give 100% to reach it. The adventure in reaching the goal is most of the fun. Secondly, to my wife and love of my life, Dana, who encouraged me to have fun with the book and for always being there and supporting this crazy dream of mine. She was my editor and 99% of the time her advice was spot on.

Foreword

I met Clifford Annis several years ago during his visit to Dr. Konstantin Frank Winery. I was immediately impressed by Clifford's passion and knowledge about Arnie Esterer. Clifford said that he planned on writing a book about Arnie's contribution to the Ohio wine industry and I was excited to see it. After reading this book I am very pleased with the results and I believe it adds a great deal to educating wine lovers about the Eastern U.S. wine renaissance and Arnie's contributions to Ohio's wine industry.

When I met Clifford I gave him a book written about my grandfather, Dr. Konstantin Frank. The book called, "Finger Lakes Wine and the Legacy of Dr. Konstantin Frank", is written by Tom Russ. I felt this book would give Clifford some good information about Dr. Frank that would help him better understand his contributions and history.

I met Arnie during his early visits to Dr. Frank's Winery. I was still a student and would spend my vacations working at the winery and vineyards learning from Konstantin. I was always amazed at how Konstantin had assembled this group he called his Cooperators. They were his disciples that learned from him and then spread the Vinifera vine growing techniques to other Eastern states. This group included: Doug Moorhead in Pennsylvania, Arnie Esterer In Ohio, Brother David Petry in Indiana,

George Matheson in Massachusetts, Elisabeth Furness in Virginia and Al Wiederkehr in Arkansas.

In later years additional cooperators were added and many of them worked with Dr. Frank during harvest in the vineyards and wine cellar and often purchased their grafted vines from his nursery. He also sold grape juice to many winemakers in the early years before their own vineyards began to produce. Konstantin was very giving with his knowledge to his Cooperators because he wanted the Eastern Wine Industry to prosper and produce better quality wines from the Vinifera grapes.

Arnie was one of Konstantin's favorite cooperators and he was very proud of his accomplishments with Markko Vineyards in Ohio. Arnie carried on Konstantin's message and techniques to another generation of Ohio vintners and helped the industry prosper. Arnie's admiration for Konstantin was mutual as evidenced by the special Markko Vineyards label called Homage Chardonnay dedicated to Dr. Frank.

Our family is grateful to all of Konstantin's Cooperators who helped spread the Vinifera movement across the Eastern United States. Today all 50 states have wineries and this has allowed more Americans to visit local wineries and learn more about wines. The U.S. has become the largest market for wines in the world. I believe this growth can be traced to the expansion of regional wineries that have allowed more Americans to learn more about wine and visit wineries nearby.

I hope you enjoy reading about Arnie as much as I did.

Cheers,
Frederick Frank
President
Dr. Konstantin Frank Winery

Introduction

In researching the story of Arnie Esterer and Markko Vineyard, it was pretty obvious that not much had been written. I found only one book on Ohio wineries but discovered a few mentions in some wine guides, a few blogs, and scattered articles here and there. When it came to Markko Vineyard, I discovered a few more one page articles written over the last 20 years, pretty much all saying the same things; Markko started in 1968, they make vinifera wines, and so on. I decided to make this an oral history or biography of Arnie and Markko Vineyard told primarily through one man's voice, that of Arnie himself, and the people who knew him best.

What lead me to consider writing a wine book? It started when I began to enjoy the "fruits of the vine" around 1999. The job I had at that time took me all over the world and about that time, I had my first visit to Australia and, like many others, fell in love with the land "down under". The site I was visiting was kind enough to schedule a wine tour for me one Sunday up in the Hunter Valley which is about 2 hours north of Sydney. The tour van held about 10 of us – some wine experts, some novices, and me, who honestly had no real knowledge of wine. I didn't know the difference between Merlot and Shiraz let alone how to spell Shiraz or pronounce it. The first winery we visited was a little one named Pepper Tree. I remember the young lady who greeted us was pleasant, friendly and always smiling. It was clear she loved her job. She poured me a glass of a 1997 Coonawarra/Hunter

Valley Shiraz and I fell in love...with the wine. I thought to myself "this is something I can get use to"...drinking wonderful wine and meeting fascinating people. We visited a number of other wineries that day and no matter where we were, everyone was having a great time...not a sour puss in the bunch.

Let's fast forward to the summer of 2014. While attending my cousin Chris's wedding in Hammondsport, NY, the heart of the Finger Lake wine region, my wife and I took the opportunity to stop in at some of our favorite wineries as well as a couple of new ones. At one of the wineries, I picked up a copy of the book *Summer in a Glass – The Coming of Age of Winemaking in the Finger Lakes* by Evan Dawson. I had discussed on and off with my wife about writing a book regarding the Ohio Winemakers and basically telling their story. I think she thought it was a bit of a pipe dream but indulged me as I rambled on. After reading Evan's book, it was clear to me it was something I needed to do. Evan did a masterful job of telling the stories of the Finger Lakes winemakers/growers and allowing their voices to come to life in his writings. Evan's book really inspired me to tell the story of a certain Ohio winemaker, in a region which is mostly overlooked - a winemaker who is clearly producing wines that can compete with the top regions in the United States if not the world.

In order to appreciate this Ohio winemaker and the challenges he faced, you have to understand his story, what drove him to become a winemaker, what brought him to a certain location/region to make the "fruit of the Gods" and the love and passion he had to produce wines that make Markko customers smile. This is the story of one remarkable man and his passion to produce only the best vinifera wines in a region where the critics said it could not be done. As a pioneer of Ohio's modern wine industry, he planted *vitis vinifera* (vinifera) varieties in Ohio back when others didn't think it possible to grow European-style wine grapes in Lake Erie's cool climate. Sound familiar? No, this is not Dr. Konstantin Frank's story. This is the story of

Arnie Esterer, Markko Vineyard's story and, for the most part, it's told in Arnie's own words. Arnie is very intelligent with a rapid fire brain. I did my best to relay his stories accurately.

Arnie "Father of vinifera in Ohio" Esterer and Me
– Photography courtesy of Jim Messenheimer 18-Jul-2018

Table of Contents

CHAPTER 1

Markko Vineyard – An Overview

AT THE END of a desolate dirt road in Conneaut, Ohio lies a true gem of Ohio wineries. Large stone pillars (see Picture 1) and a stone sign greet you as the forest canopy covers the dirt road leading up to a small 19th century looking Moonshiner building, the home of Markko Vineyards. The building itself is affectionately referred to as "the shack in the back" (see Picture 2). Two large, as Arnie likes to call them, purebred "Markko dogs" (75% old English sheepdog and 25% bearded collie) will greet you most of time with smiles and wagging tails. One should not be fooled by the outside appearance of the winery as you have just arrived at a place full of rustic ambiance and delicious wines.

Picture 1: Markko Vineyard circa 2015
– Photograph courtesy of Markko Vineyard

Picture 2: Markko Vineyard Tasting Room and Wine Cellar
– Photography courtesy of Jim Messenheimer

Markko Vineyard was founded April 17, 1968 by Arnie Esterer and his late partner, Tim Hubbard. Markko represents one of the first serious attempts by an Ohio winemaker to grow European vinifera grapes on the shores of Lake Erie. Markko is hands down a winery consistently producing some of finest vinifera wines in the Buckeye state, if not all of the country for more than 50 years. Please note, this is not just my own personal opinion. Over the past four plus years of researching for this book, the hundreds of wine lovers I have spoken to reinforce the excellence of Markko's vinifera wines. Many speak of the "pilgrimage" they make just to visit with Arnie, sip some delightful wines paired with Markko Gouda cheese and to reminisce about the late Tim Hubbard, Arnie's former partner, and Linda Frisbie, the former winery manager. Visitors often go home with a case of wine making the trip, in some cases from as far away as Florida and California, all worth it.

Markko Vineyard's focus has always been on growing and making wine from vinifera grapes. With guidance from Dr. Konstantin Frank starting in the late 1960's up until Dr. Frank's passing on September 6, 1985, Arnie and Tim built a winery that has led the way for the next generation of vinifera growers and winemakers in Ohio. Markko did not happen overnight. It took years of trials and errors, successes and failures and much collaboration and learning. Arnie put it best when he said "The potential is great here. Markko is an experiment on what you could do, how to do it, who could do it, and what grapes to focus on. When I first started I thought we could do it in 25 years and now its 50 years and we're still not quite there." Arnie expanded saying "Markko is a giant experiment…as a demonstration of some particular way of doing things. It's a combination of Dr. Frank, Arnie Esterer, Tim Hubbard, Linda Frisbee, and all the options we had in between. If other people can learn from our mistakes or learn from our successes and if we make a success and they follow it, that's a complement but it is also one way to move ahead."

For Arnie and Tim to consider starting Markko Vineyard in northeast Ohio, you need to understand why this area is so conducive to growing grapes and, in particular, the vinifera varietals.

Lake Erie Appellation – Why grow vinifera here?

In Leon Adam's book *The Wines of America*[1], Leon writes about the long history of wine in Ohio, starting back with the first plantings of grape vines by Nicholas Longworth around 1823 on Bald Hill overlooking the Ohio River in Cincinnati. According to Leon, Ohio was the premier wine producing state by 1859, with nearly 570,000 gallons yearly.

From Toledo to Buffalo and the wine islands of Lake Erie (e.g.. Bass Island, Put-in-Bay and Kelley's Island), grape growers have planted Concord, Catawba and other native grapes for winemaking for hundreds of years. According to a recent release from the Ohio Department of Agriculture, Ohio's grape growers and winemaking industry has a $1.3 billion dollar impact on the state's economy annually. The number of wineries in the state of Ohio as of September 12, 2017 was 265, a 51% increase over 175 in 2012. Additionally, Ohio is the 6th largest wine producer in the country and the 9th largest grape producer with 1,500 acres.[2] I'm not going to write about the history of winemaking in Ohio. I do recommend, however, either the Philip R. Hines book *The Wines and Wineries of Ohio*[3] or the Leon Adams book *The Wines of America*[1] which discuss in detail the history of wine and winemaking in Ohio.

Webster's dictionary defines Appellation as "an identifying name or title" or "the act of calling by name".[4] Therefore, appellation is a term that identifies the location where the grapes were grown, fermentation of the grapes to wine and finally the bottling and sale of the wine. All of these activities are occurring in a specific location/geographical area; its place of origin.

It wasn't until the late 1960's that the growing of vinifera grapes commenced in earnest in Ohio, particularly in northeastern Ohio in what is today called the Lake Erie Appellation. Arnie was once asked by Steve Corso on a visit to Markko Vineyard, as written in the article in Edible Cleveland in the fall 2013[5], "So you were one of the first wineries in the area to make wine from vinifera grapes?" Arnie answered "The first".

According to the Ohio Grape Industries Committee website[6], "The Lake Erie American Viticultural Area (AVA) is the region that includes 2,236,800 acres (905,200 ha) of land on the south shore of Lake Erie in the U.S. states of Ohio, New York, and Pennsylvania. Over 42,000 acres (17,000 ha) of the region are planted in grapevines. Grapes were first cultivated in the area in the early 19th century, and many wineries survived Prohibition in the 20th century by legally selling grapes to home winemakers or illegally selling wine to consumers in Canada."

The Lake Erie viticultural region (Lake Erie Appellation) has a 185+ year history of grape growing and winemaking. Through trial and error over the years, the region has proven it can support the growing of vinifera grapes. According to Arnie Esterer, the one geographical feature that defines and distinguishes the Lake Erie viticultural region from its surroundings is the presence of Lake Erie. As Arnie said to me during one of our many interviews, "The proximity of Lake Erie and the influence it exerts on the local climate is the fundamental factor that permits commercially successful viticulture in this area."

The temperature, especially the length of the frost-free growing season, is a key determining factor in the viability of a vineyard in the northeastern United States. T.D. Jordan and T. J. Zabalda stated in the bulletin *Cultural Practices for Commercial Vineyards*[7] that:

> "Temperature is the first consideration in selecting the location of a vineyard. It involves length of growing season, as well as magnitude and frequency of winter minimums. Temperature requirements must be satisfied for a site to be considered."

Jordan and Zabalda go on to note that a commercial vineyard in the ideal region need a growing season of at least 165 days whereas 185+ days is preferable. The winter minimum temperature should infrequently fall below -10°F and never below -15°F.

Markko Vineyard – Why Conneaut?

With all this said, the location of Markko Vineyard was carefully selected by Arnie Esterer and Tim Hubbard because of its proximity to Lake Erie, the 185+ day growing season, the ideal soils and the wide and rapid seasonal fluctuation of the lake's water temperature.

This fluctuation's lag with respect to seasonal air temperature varia-tions, serves a very beneficial climatologic effect throughout the year. The accumulation of ice and the very cold water of the lake serves to cool the climate of the adjacent land against early spring warm spells which would otherwise force premature development of buds and thereby leave the grapevines vulnerable to freeze damage. In late spring, the lake commences to warm rapidly and then buffers the grapevines against late spring frost. The warm summer temperature of the lake is carried into the fall, warming the air adjacent to the lake and keeping fall frosts at bay. The proximity to the lake in winter af-fords considerable protection against extreme cold temperatures

The results, according to Arnie, are a 185 day growing season at Markko Vineyard which is ideal for vinifera grapevines. As Arnie has told anyone who wants to listen, vinifera grows well at Markko due to the location, location, location…and the location. As the French say, it's the terrior…the combination of soil, climate and variety of grape. According to many wine journals and dictionaries, terror "is the set of all environmental factors that affect a crop's phenotype, including unique environment contexts, farming practices and a crop's specific growth habitat. Collectively, these contextual characteristics are said to have a character; *terroir* also refers to this character."[8]

Arnie believes that the best place in Ohio to grow vinifera is the Lake Erie Appellation. When a Lake Erie designation is indicated on the label of a wine, it means that the grapes used in the wine came from this specific viticulture area which has its own terrior. In the November 16, 2018 *The Gadding Vine*[9], which is Markko's newslet-ter that is published monthly, Arnie discussed the need to modify the Lake Erie appellation. Arnie wrote:

> "The Lake Erie appellation now needs three sub-appellations
> - Grand River, Conneaut Creek and Isle St George. These
> wine appellations stay important as winegrowers find the

"personalities" of their wines in each as their vintages develop. Over many years these consistent traits justify characterization with a name. In copying the French system use in the world, it all seems to work. Hopefully it helps guide wine lovers and tasters who look.

Each winegrower around the world doing grapes of Burgundy begin to see how far these wines have come . . . . . and how they can grow. Beginners to experts of wine will find interest in new wines as each winemaker captures what's called Terroir - the unique nose and palate you sense. The "Terroir" of each vineyard stands alone, and only identifies itself over a number of years as the unique factors of soil, climate and the winemaker manifest themselves in each bottle and variety.

It's here now and will continue through the years as oenophiles continue following each vintage and its life. Some national press always helps.

May you all enjoy the best in wine exploring "The Creek" here along the Lake."[9]

Part of the vision and dream for Markko Vineyard comes with the concept of terroir of the Conneaut Creek appellation. This concept sums up wines unique character which comes from conditions which man cannot control. A vineyard's terrior appears as each vintage reveals its character. These characteristics include color, aroma, bouquet, body, tannins, complexities and overall balance. Only grapes, year after year, from the same vineyard bring out these subtle variations. These form the essence of estate bottled wines. It does not make them better or great but tells a story to enjoy. As Arnie has told me many times "the wine speaks for itself".

During a visit on August 31, 2015, Arnie said to me "Cliff, you're writing a history of why Markko is important...not a biography." However, without Arnie there is no Markko. Arnie stated "Tim Hubbard saw that we could grow wine grapes in this region...would be good for the region. We are on the same Latitude of Rome, Italy here. Still learning on how we grow grapes here...still need to figure out a vinifera grape varietal for this region. We are a generation away from figuring that out and how to make it and grow in this climate and soil...another generation at least." I beg to differ with Arnie on this point. In the 50+ years of Markko, Arnie has figured it out...the rest of the winemakers just need to listen and learn.

CHAPTER **2**

The History: The Road to a Cooperator of Dr. Konstantin Frank

IT WAS MARCH 25, 2016 and I was walking out to the vineyard with Arnie. That day was the first time that Arnie opened up about his past, his roots; the pre-winemaking days. Arnie is a private man when it comes to his family and the past. It has taken a while for him to talk about where he came from and what led to 1968 and his decision to become a professional winemaker. I credit some of his opening up to the building of a friendship between us over time, which only makes sense to me considering the kind of man he is. You have to have trust in someone first, before a friendship can ever blossom. Arnie and I had a number of discussions about his family over the years and what evolved was a story in itself.

Arnulf, Arnie, Esterer was born on May 8, 1932 in Bochum, Germany. His sister, Alice, was born in Germany as well. When he was two years old, the family escaped Germany to Ann Arbor, Michigan. During one interview Arnie told me "The story is my mother, Marie-Louise Burt, came from an old American family in Ann Arbor. She got a BS Degree in Chemistry from the University of Michigan, and then she went on to Yale and in 1928 got a Master's Degree in Chemistry from there. She then went to Germany to do some research and there she met my Dad, Arnulf Karl Esterer, who was working for Benzoyl making gasoline out of coke. He had his Ph.D. in Chemistry from the University at Wurzburg. To make a long story short, they got married and I came along on May 8th 1932 and then my sister Alice came along. I remember my parents telling me this. We were over in Germany and my grandmother came over for a visit in 1934. My mother and father had to go vote. Remember, this is 1934 in Germany and there was a certain politician who was in charge. My parents go to the voting station and the guy hands them a ballot and a pencil and he sits back and watches them. It's time to mark the ballot and there was one name on the ballot; Adolf Hitler. When they got married, they got a copy of *Mein Kampf*. When I was about one and half years old, my grandmother brought me to Ann Arbor for a month or two and then we went back to Germany. In 1934, we left Germany for good and moved to the United States. We went back to Ann Arbor Michigan to my grandmother's house. My grandfather had died back in 1921. My grandmother's sister and her husband, Uncle Bert, lived nearby. He was "the Albert E. Green" professor of Engineering at the University of Michigan and his father was the first dean of the Engineering School. We moved in with them and my Dad went to look for a job. He applied to both Monsanto and International Paper. International Paper made him an offer and he took it. And, he regretted it. We went to Canada for the next 8 or 10 years. Monsanto had come in with an offer two weeks after he had accepted the one from International Paper. For the rest of his life he felt he should have gone with Monsanto. So, we spent a few years in Canada. My mother spoke French, English and German so no problem there."

Arnie's father was an interesting man in his own right. He authored and had eight books published after he retired as a Chemist. Arnie's father was born in Ching Tau, China in 1905 and lived there 15 years.

Arnie's grandfather was an Electrical Engineer and went there in 1900. Arnie remembered "They got there on the Trans-Siberia railroad through Russia. Grandfather was helping to electrify the coal mines in China. He was a German Electrical Engineer working for Siemens-Houskin. My dad went to a German grade school and high school in Shanghai. When the Japanese attacked Ching Tau during World War I, my grandfather help set the explosives to defend the city. The explosives didn't go off so he had to go back and reset them and was captured by the Japanese. He was sent to Japan as a prisoner of war for 7 years. Grandfather published a couple of articles on this in *Geo-Politic Magazine*, which was a magazine published in Germany. The family came back to Germany in 1919."

During one of my visits with Arnie in August 2018, Arnie took me down to the house for the first time to look at some old photo albums of the family and Arnie's childhood years in Canada. While looking at a number of old picture albums of Arnie's childhood, Arnie talked about his family time in Canada, "Here's a picture of my sister and me. My dad took great pictures. My mother's father was from West Point. Here's picture of our place in Canada…I grew up in Canada. We use to ski up there about 10 miles from town. Here's a picture of the whole family (see Picture 3). I'm the oldest. The picture is Cambridge Road in January 1939. My sibling's names are Alice and Marianna. Marianna died of pancreatic cancer. My dad was working for International Paper then. The back of the picture says January 1939, Hawkesbury, Ontario, Canada. My parents bought the house in Canada; it was a rundown place right on the Otter River in northwestern Ontario, Canada. My mother and father fixed it all up. My dad gardened there and that's where I learned. He had all kinds of flowers. Here's a picture of the pulp mill where he worked and it smelled of Sulphur dioxide. Yep, that's where I grew up and oh, I became a Canadian Boy Scout in first grade."

Picture 3: The Esterer Family circa January 1939 (left to right, Marie-Louse (mother), baby Marianna (sister) in mother's arms, Arnie, Arnulf (father) and Alice (sister)

Arnie continued to talk about his years growing up in Canada. About this time, Canada entered World War II in 1939. Arnie's father had 7 siblings and 4 were in the German army. As we were talking, Arnie said "One of my uncle's was an executive officer on a German submarine. He went up the Thymes River in England and they torpedoed a ship. The English depth charged his sub and sank it. He came to the surface and became a prisoner of war in Canada. He wrote us a letter saying, I'm a prisoner of war in Canada, I can't visit you now but I hope soon it will be possible. He came later and visited us." The visit by Arnie's uncle was not a wise move. Arnie continued "I remember Mom said to my Dad your brother is going to escape to come see you. He had sent us a postcard saying that. Mom took the postcard to the Canadian police to tell them this. Then, a guy, my uncle, shows up in a German army uniform to where my dad works asking for my father. My dad called the Canadian Mounted Police and they came to our home. My dad ended up in a prisoner of war camp in Canada so my mom and us came back to the US in 1940 or early 1941. We got a good lawyer, got my dad out of prison and brought him to the US. He then got a job in the University of Michigan's chemistry department. My dad had 40 patents in brake fluids as they were going to synthetic fluids. I finished my childhood years growing up in Michigan, graduated from University Michigan and with a degree in Economics and a minor in Russian. I got a Master's degree and then met my future wife, Katy."

Kate (Katy) Micou Esterer (February 19, 1936 – April 16, 2017) and the kids

Arnie has told me many times, Markko Vineyards success would not have been what it is today without the contributions of so many. I will talk about only a few in this book, but it is clear the first one has to be Arnie's late wife, Kate Micou Esterer (see Picture 4 below). Arnie met Kate in 1955 in Michigan and they got engaged in June/July 1955. Arnie couldn't remember the exact date, typical man. It was not long after they met Kate went to Switzerland to study singing/voice. According to Arnie, she had a wonderful voice.

Picture 4: Kate Esterer (also known as Kiki or Katy) with son Andrew Esterer

Arnie has said many times Kate was very talented. She was the first woman to deliver mail for the Post Office in Conneaut. Kate and Arnie had four children; Andrew, David, Paul and Katherine (see Picture 5). She raised all four of the children and according to Arnie "She raised them well and they are four great kids." She wrote the newsletter for Markko for many years and what a writer she was. I've included just a couple examples of Kate's wonderful ability to make words sing:

"I DREAM OF CHARDONNAY WITH A LIGHT, GOLDEN AIR . . . a little trite perhaps, but if you've tasted our 1988 Chardonnays, than you know what we're talking about." – Courtesy of "The Gadding Vine", No. 25, Fall 1990[10]

"A VINEYARD CYCLE: But wine is a challenge that never ends, because no two wines and no two seasons are ever alike. The leaves fall, the wood grows hard. The snow comes, and the naked vines stand out in the empty night, alone and unprotected. What will happen to them *this* year? What form will the pruning take in the early days of spring? Each vine must be examined and trimmed according to how well it grew the previous summer, and how well it survived the winter. Then the sap runs, the growth starts once again. No two springs proceed in the same way. Maybe it will be cold and wet, or maybe unduly warm, bringing unseasonal growth and the chance of being caught by a late frost. Will June be cool? How many sprays will we have to use to keep at bay the ever lurking bugs and blights that prey upon the vines? Will late summer be hot and dry, bringing the acid down and the sugar up to the peak of perfection? Or will it rain during the ripening period, forcing more liquid into the grape than the ripened skin can hold, causing it to burst and spill the juice on the berries below, which in turn will cause them to rot? Will the birds be kind or will they literally destroy the harvest? And what about the yellow jackets, which in their search for liquid, any liquid, punch holes in the grapes, reducing each bunch to a soggy mess? Then it is over (generally before one is quite prepared) and the grapes are in and the winemaking has begun. In most other fruit growing endeavors this is the end of the line, but with wine it is just the beginning." – Courtesy of *"The Gadding Vine"*, No. 3, Fall 1978.[11]

Picture 5: The Esterer children (left to right)
Andrew, Katherine, David and Paul

If that wasn't enough for one person to do, Kate help start two art centers, one in Ashtabula and when they moved to Conneaut, Kate and Joan Newcomb (a co-founder and former director of the Conneaut Community Center) started the Conneaut Art Center which is still going strong today. When speaking of Kate on one of my visits, Arnie said "She had incredible talents. She had few friends but the ones she had were good ones and they did wonderful things together."

When I visited Arnie on July 26, 2017, Arnie wanted to talk about Kate Esterer's final days in April 2017 before her passing. Arnie spoke with quite a bit of emotion in his voice "My ex-wife Kate fell and called my daughter. She called 911 and had many broken bones and had osteoporosis pretty bad. My daughter, Katherine, called and said she is in real trouble. So, I hopped in the truck and drove down to North Carolina Saturday night. It took me eight hours to get there. She was coming out of wrist surgery and by 6 pm she was up and perky so we had a good talk. Katherine was there so she went home for a while and Katy and talked some more. Katherine came back, so she stayed with her and I went home. Sunday morning was Easter and Kate was to have surgery at 9 o'clock in the morning. The doctor came to us and said they were going to replace her femur but she should be walking the next day. Kate agreed to go ahead with the surgery. We went to church Sunday morning and afterwards, we went to the hospital. Katherine was there but she went home and I stayed. Kate was in surgery at 9:30 am was still in surgery at 10:30 am. Then the nurse came out and said the doctor wanted to talk to me. The doctor told me Kate is dying and she will be gone soon. There were bone fragments in the leg and her blood pressure was falling and they can't keep her alive. I have to tell my daughter. Katherine came back and I told her that her mother was dying. We got the family together. It's around noon time so we needed to talk to Kate because we're going to lose her soon. I went in to talk to Kate and she could still hear us. We, the family, are all around her. I put my hand on her head and we are all talking to her and we watched the blood pressure go down and down. Finally, I send to her "Kate, you can let go". Within 20 seconds her blood pressure went to zero and then she was gone. We went up to Canada to spread some of her ashes…300 miles due north of Markko at the north channel of Lake Heron. We spread her ashes in the bay and they went right to the bottom. That is where Kate and I got engaged. We celebrated her funeral at the lake…that is what Kate wanted. She only wanted family and friends to come. Kate was 81 when she passed. We were married 37 good years and I miss her every day."

Arnie and Kate had three sons, Andrew (born 1962), David (born 1964) and Paul (born 1967) and one daughter Katherine (born 1969). Paul was interested in the wine business at one time. Arnie and Paul went into a partnership around 2011-2012 but things didn't go as exactly as planned. Arnie said "It didn't move as fast as he wanted it to. He was looking at it as a business kind of thing…its more than just a business, at least in my book it is. It helps to have passion. I wanted it to be a family business. It was really my fault it didn't work. I'm just too stubborn." Arnie then said "you can't make decisions in just one generation. I wanted to be like the Frank family in New York, they will soon start the 4th generation. I always saw this as a family business but it might not work out that way." As of the publishing of this book, Katherine, Arnie's daughter, lives in North Carolina; Paul is in Chagrin Falls Ohio, David in Columbus Ohio and Andrew in St. Louis. In spite of the potential that the second generation might not take over, the love Arnie has for his family and his wine family is clear.

On one of my numerous visits to Markko back in August 2018, Arnie's son David payed an unexpected visit. I was able to sit down with David and talk about his life growing up at Markko. During our discussion, I asked David what he would want people to know about his dad. David sat for a minute, remember he wasn't expecting to be interviewed, and recalled "I was 4 or 5 when we moved here, 1967, 1968 or 1969. It was kind of scary moving out to the middle of nowhere. The nights are as dark as you can see with no lights but there was just pure enjoyment seeing all the cool stuff we could do in the woods during the day and night too. We would camp out with my brothers and build dirt tracks for our bikes to race. I think all of us would say it was a pretty cool place to grow up. We were just outdoor kids. There weren't the distractions of technology that are around today. There were other things you just did outside and first it got to be like helping out in the wine cellar or just mowing the yard or just being a boy. I loved to work with any kind of machine or tool; it's something that was pretty cool. Once we got to a certain age, we were able to drive the tractor which was the ultimate…

that was the thing. He would spell it out for us, this is what you're going to get to do and the next thing you can do once you are ready. Once you can drive the tractor, okay what jobs can you do? Can you mow the grass? Can you spray? There was a different level of complexity with specific jobs and that was the kind of thing my brothers and I would compete with. I was like hey guess what I got to do today? Those things I definitely remember. At the time, we didn't understand what an Estate Winery meant as far as growing the grapes, making the wine, bottling and labeling, marketing and selling it. It wasn't anything that dawned on us, it was just the way it was and we had nothing else to bench mark it against. We thought everyone did it that way not realizing that we were in a special place to be able to have that exposure to everything. I helped plant some of the vines that are out there now and watched them grow and nurtured them; that was part of the process. You'd do the work, taking care of them in the summer to picking and bottling, crushing and the whole thing in the fall. It was always a lot of fun I think."

While I had David there, I decided to ask him, what I thought was a very important question. If Markko were to cease to exist today, what is the one thing you want people to remember? David said "I think one of the things that drove Dad was to be a pioneer, to be the first to do something, to try something that people said couldn't be done. It's almost like being a coach of a team because you could have almost the exact same players but the conditions will be different. In this case, the weather is different, the climates is different from year to year. I will never forget when I was little and I went to one of the first wine tastings and someone asked what the difference between the '94 and the '95 was and he would say a year. It's been different weather, different climate and there are all these different variables like the kind of winter it was, how much moisture we got, and did we have the huge dips which is hardest on the grapes going from really warm to really cold. If it got cold it was fine as long as it got steadily cold not getting really warm and then cold again. Those are things I remember as far as feeding into that same feeling that every year is different with a different set of problems which led to an experiment or, as Dad said, an ongoing research project/experiment."

In the Navy and finally Ohio

About the time Arnie and Kate were engaged in 1956, Arnie had accepted a job with Union Carbide and moved to Ashtabula, Ohio. Kate finished up her studies in Switzerland and moved back to Michigan in January 1956. Kate and Arnie got married that same month and off to Ashtabula they went. They rented a house and settled into married life, well at least that's what they thought. Arnie sent the draft board a notice that he was married, figuring this would keep him from being drafted. However, at the end of February 1956, Arnie got a letter telling him to report for the draft at 5:30 am (Arnie couldn't remember the exact date) in March 1956 and boom, he's in the Navy. Kate packed up and moved in with Arnie's parents in Ann Arbor, Michigan. Their first stop in Ohio was a bit short lived.

In March 1956, Arnie went to Detroit for his Navy physical. The Navy sent Arnie to Washington, DC for a year to study code breaking and then off to Officer Candidate School (OCS). Arnie recalled "I went to OCS. I wanted to be in intelligence, code breaking, and they sent me to the Naval Communication Station." After OCS, Arnie was stationed in Japan for two years. Arnie chuckled "I went to Japan (Yokohama) carrying confidential information. Imagine, me carrying confidential stuff. I was sent to northern Japan, the Island of Hokkaido, as the officer in charge of 15 sailors watching the Russians. Kate came over and was in Japan with me and we did a lot of skiing there. We'd climb up the mountain, have lunch and ski down. What a life!"

In 1959, Arnie's service in the Navy was up so Arnie and Kate moved back to Ashtabula and Arnie returned to work for Union Carbide. Before starting back with Union Carbide, Arnie and Kate went to Germany with his Dad for a family reunion. Arnie recalled "When I went to Germany with the family, there were all these wines, wonderful wines. I think the wine bug really hit me then."

In the early-to-mid 1960's, Arnie Esterer (see Picture 6 below) was working for Union Carbide in Ashtabula, Ohio. Arnie first started thinking of a winery around 1965. Arnie stated "A number of people at the plant were farming and drinking wine. People were growing grapes around here but no one was making wine…which got me to the idea of making wine. All of our friends started making wine and we'd get together for parties and tasting each other's wine." It was through these wine gatherings and friendships, that Arnie was introduced to Doug Moorhead and Bill Konnerth (co-founders of Presque Isle Wine Cellars) and to vinifera wines. As Arnie will tell you "They lead me to Dr. Konstantin Frank. Doug was a cooperator of Dr. Frank's."

Picture 6: Arnie Esterer

Arnie was reading books about winemaking, viniculture and had numerous discussions about wine with Doug Moorhead. One day, Arnie discovered a book called *A Wine-Growers Guide*[12] by Phillip Wagner on winemaking and that was what finally set in motion Arnie's desire for making his own wine from grapes he grew. Irony can be a funny thing. Arnie's uncle on his mother's side was a childhood friend of Phillip Wagner. Arnie thought maybe fate had something to do with him finding Wagner's book or maybe just dumb luck. Whatever the case, Arnie asked himself "What could this region do? It's a good grape growing region...a super region. At one time there were 24,000 acres of grapes growing in Ohio." Arnie always felt he was a "square peg in a round hole" in his job at Union Carbide, so he made the momentous decision to leave his job and become a winemaker full-time.

Arnie heard about Dr. Frank from Doug Moorhead and Philip Wagner. Both men encouraged him that if he was serious about being a winemaker, meeting Dr. Frank was essential, leading Arnie to write Dr. Frank about coming to visit.

A Cooperator of Dr. Konstantin Frank... "Who are you, a somebody or a nobody?"

The meeting between Arnie and Dr. Konstantin Frank (see Picture 7) back in 1967 was one of the most important events for the Ohio wine industry; it just wasn't known back then exactly how their collaboration and friendship would impact vinifera grape growing and winemaking in Ohio.

Picture 7: Dr. Konstantin Frank – Photograph courtesy of the Frank Family

In October 1967, Arnie's wife, Kate, told him one morning over break-fast that if he was serious and wanted to be in the wine business, he needed to go work in a winery. Arnie had planted some Chardonnay vines in the backyard, but that was about as far as it went on the growing front. With a couple of weeks of vacation coming, Arnie said "She was absolutely right so I packed my bags and drove over to the Finger Lakes."

Arnie got to Hammondsport, NY around midnight and checked into the Hammondsport Hotel. He got the owner out of bed which, let's just say, didn't make the man happy. The owner asked Arnie his reasons for visiting Hammondsport. Arnie told him he was going to meet with Dr. Konstantin Frank. The owner said "Oh, the cuckoo up on the hill that makes wine."

Arnie got up at 7:00 am the next morning and drove to every winery; Taylor, Bully Hill, etc. and everything was closed (remember in the late 1960's, there weren't that many wineries to visit). Arnie arrived at Dr. Frank's about quarter to eight and was standing out in the parking lot when Dr. Frank's wife, Eugenia, came outside and looked at Arnie and said "Are you looking for the doctor?" Arnie said "Yes Ma'am." She told Arnie the doctor is having a cup of coffee and will be right out. Arnie decided to wander around a few minutes looking at the tanks and the equipment. Dr. Frank came out with his hat, purple boots and apron and waved for Arnie to come his way. They walked into the winery with Arnie close behind and as they entered into the stacks of wine, Dr. Frank stopped dead in his tracks, turned around and said to Arnie, "Who are you, a somebody or a nobody?" Arnie thought carefully and quickly as he knew his answer could make or break everything. Arnie said "I'm a nobody." Dr. Frank said "Good, let's go to work." Arnie told me many times that Dr. Frank had a good sense of people and in that first meeting, he felt Dr. Frank saw something in him...a student of vinifera, or as Dr. Frank called them, his cooperators.

Dr. Frank showed Arnie around the winery and the cellar and immediately put Arnie to work on Pinot Noir. Arnie worked at Dr. Frank's for a full week, pressing Pinot Noir and punching down Cabernet. He pressed Chardonnay and Riesling as well. As Arnie put it "I was a gopher or what they affectionately call today a cellar rat."

One night during that first visit, Arnie was sitting by the press around midnight and he said to Dr. Frank "I would like to start a small winery, maybe 30 or 40 acres." Immediately, without hesitation, Dr. Frank said "No no, you need 100 acres." Arnie didn't want to be that big and he argued on and off with Dr. Frank that night. As Arnie put it "That argument was a one-way street and remember, I'm the nobody."

During that week, a lot of important wine people came by to see Dr. Frank. Craig Churchill was buying wine for American Airlines and dropped by. Peter Sichel, a writer and educator from Germany who worked at the Cornell Research Center, showed up and was talking to Dr. Frank about the harvest. As Arnie said "It was a who's who of the wine industry coming to visit him."

Dr. Frank educated Arnie on vinifera that first week. Arnie said "Dr. Frank told me there are five (5) great wine grapes, Chardonnay, Pinot Noir, Cabernet Sauvignon, Riesling and Pinot Gris. I asked Dr. Frank which was the greatest and he said Pinot Gris. Why did Dr. Frank say Pinot Gris? All the others had a home, but no country has the signature grape of Pinot Gris. Dr. Frank was thinking of the United States to have signature grape for our region…he was way ahead of us". Recently in late 2017, a number of the winemakers/growers in the Lake Erie Appellation from Geneva to Conneaut, Ohio met to discuss a signature grape for their area. The grape being bantered around was Pinot Gris, ergo Dr. Frank was ahead of his time.

The most important take away Arnie brought back from Dr. Frank at the end of that first week was Dr. Frank's insistence about the purchase of land. As Arnie said, "The only thing I left with was the idea that I have to buy 100 acres. So, I came back home and started looking for land." Arnie knew that without the 100 acres, getting his hands on vinifera cuttings from Dr. Frank's vineyard was clearly not going to happen. Arnie didn't go away empty handed; he got a 5 gallon carboy of Pinot Noir for his efforts. Upon returning home, the priority was to find a plot of 100 acres that had the right terrior.

Arnie's quest for the right location for a vineyard led him to a parcel of land owned by Leo Markko of Chicago situated in Conneaut, Ohio. Arnie visited the land and liked what he saw. Now came the fun part, well not really. It was time to make an offer on the parcel. Around that same time, Arnie ran into Tim Hubbard (see Picture 8). Arnie had known Tim for a number of years and one day while in his office talking about stocks he said to him "I've started home winemaking and I said I think this would be good region for wine making and Tim agreed." Arnie said "I was bidding $6,000 to $8,000 to $10,000… someone told me if you're buying land, send a contract with all the details and include a check for earnest money. Then all they have to do is sign the contract. I called Leo Markko with a first offer of

$14,000 per acre for 130 acres and he still said no." Arnie told all this to Tim and asked him "Do you want to go together on this and he said yes. Tim agreed it was good project and he became a partner." As Arnie put it "he brought moral and financial support. I was the majority owner (51%) and Tim (49%) the minority owner. Our lawyer told us someone has to be the boss and it was decided it was me."

*Picture 8: Tim Hubbard (right) and his cousin Warner Bacon;
Picture taken July 27, 2008*

Arnie continued about Tim "Tim drank wine and was a man about town. He was a stock broker and sold bonds in Erie, PA. Tim saw the future in the grapes for this area whether we were successful or not."

25

Arnie and Tim drew up a contract and mailed it off to Leo Markko and his two sisters. Apparently the sisters liked what they saw and Leo agreed to sell to Arnie and Tim. That date was April 17, 1968 which from then on would be known at Markko Vineyards and to their loyal followers as Founder's Day. Arnie finished by saying "We started the partnership in 1968. We stayed partners and good friends until he died." I asked Arnie if he named the winery after Leo Markko and he smiled and said "I followed the Boordy's guide from Phillip Wagner. Good wineries had double letters, such as Boordy with two O's and Gallo with the two L's. It was the Markko land and just a good name, nothing else. Markko lives on when I'm gone, not Arnie's winery."

Later in the spring of 1968 with 130 acres in hand, Arnie and Tim drove over to see Dr. Frank. Arnie and Tim communicated to Dr. Frank they had the 100+ acres and needed 2,000 vines. Arnie said Dr. Frank was blunt and to the point "No, 500 vines!" Arnie continued "He would not let me buy more. I argued and argued that whole weekend and still I went home with 500 vines. So, we planted the 500 vines. I went back the next year and bought another 500 vines and every year we went back. We would work the whole weekend making grafts. He would look at them and we'd put them in the box and so that's how that went. After 10 years we had 5,000 vines in the ground."

Arnie stated that the two most important decisions they made by listening to Dr. Frank over those 10 years was the vineyard had to be 100 acres and to start small. Dr. Frank had a message about hybrid grapes, "get rid of them". If you have second rate grapes, like hybrids, you get second rate wine.

Early in 2018, I asked Arnie what was the most important thing Dr. Frank taught him. Arnie didn't hesitate and said "What kind of wine you're going to make in the end, how to make the best and how to find the terrior and he kept us focused on the five great wine grapes: Chardonnay, Riesling, Cabernet Sauvignon, Pinot Noir and Pinot Gris.

I asked Dr. Frank many times which was the best one and he'd always say Pinot Gris. In a way, that's what we are doing here. He gave us that focus. Pinot Gris really does not have a home. So Chardonnay is Burgundy and Pinot Noir, maybe Pinot is the grape for this terroir. However, the most important lesson was don't accept doctrine, whatever the academic or Cornell tells you. He was always looking at research and the work he had done over the years. He was in a new country establishing a new vinicultural appellation and he had to prove that vinifera could do it. That's what we are doing here in Ohio, proving vinifera can grow and make great wines."

October 1967 was the start of a more than 50 year friendship between Arnie and Dr. Frank and the Frank family. The friendship lasts to this day and so does the admiration and love.

Philip M. Wagner (1904 – 1997)

The story of Arnie and Markko Vineyard would not be possible without the guidance from and friendship with Philip M. Wagner. Philip M. Wagner founded Maryland's best-known winery, Boordy Vineyards in 1945, and introduced French-American hybrid grapes to America.[1] Boordy Vineyards was run by Philip and Jocelyn Wagner until they sold the name and equipment in 1980 but they continued to run the nursery to supply their hybrid vines to growers nationwide.[12] I asked Arnie what impact Philip Wagner had on him and Markko Vineyard. Arnie smiled and said "He had a huge impact on me. His writings, how to grow grapes…it doesn't matter what grapes you're growing, he was pushing hybrids. I read his book and it was so well written; it was my guide to growing grapes and winemaking. Everything that he did was okay, it did not matter what kind of grape. Then I went to Dr. Frank and he said no hybrids. If you're going to make wine you might as well do the best and work on vinifera. Dr. Frank's idea was to grow the best that you can grow. The vision we had for Markko Vineyard has been influenced by Dr. Frank and Philip Wagner. I bought Dr. Frank's ideas and bought everything of Wagner except his promotion of hybrids. I bought all kinds of winery equipment from him. I bought a bottling machine and filter pads. I bought Wagner's growing techniques, his schedule, what time of year you do it, what best practices are and why you do it. He was an elegant writer. He was the editor of the Baltimore Sun and this winery he had, was a part-time job for him. Every time someone comes in here and wants to start a winery I say take this book, *A Wine-Growers Guide*[13]. Arnie continued "The interesting thing was I was introduced to Dr. Frank by the hybrid guy, Phillip Wagner, Dr. Frank's alter ego. I read about Dr. Frank. Wagner wrote the wine growers guide and in the back of the book he talked about Dr. Frank in Hammondsport trying to do vinifera. Phillip was a friend of my uncle who came from Ann Arbor, Michigan, my hometown. They played together and were buddies. I would go down to Washington D.C. to sell wine and do tastings. I did a tasting on Constitution Avenue for a lot of State Department people. I would come through Towson, Maryland and visit him. Last time I talked with him he was 92 sitting in his office still selling equipment." Philip Wagner passed away in 1997 not long after Arnie's last conversation with him.

After Arnie returned from his visit with Dr. Frank in October 1967, he sent Arnie to California in late 1967 to meet André Tchelistcheff or as Dr. Frank told Arnie, "the Maestro" and "the father of California winemaking". He was Dr. Frank's old friend whom he had met on trips to California in the 1960's when he was working for Gold Seal.

André Tchelistcheff (December 7, 1901 – Apri 5, 1994) – "The Maestro"

André Tchelistcheff (see Picture 9) has been referred to by many as the "Dean of American Winemaking".[14] André Tchelistcheff was hired by the famous Georges de Latour and joined Beaulieu Vineyards in 1938. As documented in *Complete Napa Valley California Wine History from Early 1800s to Today*, "André Tchelistcheff was responsible for introducing many of the modern wine making techniques that were used in Europe."[15] Furthermore, it states "André Tchelistcheff pioneered the need for proper sanitation and the use of small, French oak barrels for aging of the wine…André Tchelistcheff introduced modern, viticulture practices of Europe. He began replanting the vineyards with higher levels of density, reducing the amount of sulfur used in the vineyards and more importantly, André Tchelistcheff focused on planting high quality French grape varietals."[15] André's significant contributions and influence on the California winemakers after Prohibition allowed for the tremendous improvement in the quality of wines which impacted all of the United States.

Picture 9: Picture of André Tchelistcheff – Photograph courtesy of the website http://www.thewinecellarinsider.com/california-wine/california-wine-history-from-early-plantings-in-1800s-to-today/[15]

Arnie's California Visit – Lessons Learned

Arnie served in the Naval reserves for 26 years and as luck would have it, he was scheduled for training duty in California, north of San Francisco in late 1967. Arnie recalled "Sonoma to my left, NAPA to the right. I drove up Highway 29 to all these wineries and there I met Sam Sebastiani of Sebastiani Vineyard and he took me on a tour at night. I went to Beaulieu to watch them pressing Cabernet with a Willmes Press, which is the same press I have, and there I met André Tchelistcheff one morning. He greeted me in his laboratory coat and we talked about how to make red wine. Tchelistcheff said we are planting some nice Pinot Noir in the Calaveras Region. Tchelistcheff was the one who did it. All red wines are better blended…the earlier you blend the better…blend in the press…better to grow them together…this is what he taught me and frankly taught the wine industry. Markko planted 85% Cabernet, 5% Chambourcin, 5% Merlot and 5% Cab Franc. The only hybrid was Chambourcin because it doesn't promote leaf form of phylloxera. That's why we planted it with root stock that is resistant to phylloxera. 500 vines are a half acre. We planted 500 vines every year so we were at 10 acres. The big thing is you have to ask questions to learn…how you ask the question is how you determine the answer. I asked Tchelistcheff a lot of questions."

The Markko Crew – Family too

Arnie told me numerous times over my many visits that Markko would not have been the success it was without his immediate family's help and, of course, the day-to-day work of the wine family or as they are better known, The Markko Crew. No winery can run with just a winemaker. You need a labor force willing to do the back breaking jobs, such as planting, pruning, picking, cleaning, moving 50 gallon barrels, cutting down trees, etc. When I spoke with Greg Johns, who is the retired Director of the Ohio State University Grape Research Center, back in August of 2018, Greg put it best "There could have been lots of books written about the people that have come and gone from Markko, and not only those folks who have come and gone but those who have stayed. Culetta Burdette is still here for 30 plus years. Even Linda's mom worked here, Linda's grandson works here now…in some cases five generations. This is a very depressed area and it's hard to find jobs; hard to find good jobs. This here at Markko is a good job, you're outside, it's good honest work and if people get frustrated or fed up or whatever it is and if they're gone for 1 day, 2 days, 20 days, they know they still have a home here and can still come back."

Arnie treats his work force like family. Most employers are quick to fire and, in some cases, never give a second chance. That is not true of Arnie. Back in August 2015, Arnie I were discussing the crew. Arnie recalled, "Early on it was obvious, we needed a labor force. We needed a crew that knows what to do and when to do it. We are, in some cases, on fourth and fifth generation workers here. Linda (Frisbie) was here 40 years, her mother, Helen Tenney, worked two years. Lucilla Kelly was vineyard manager for 20 years." Arnie laughed and said "She had a big mouth. She would get on the crew but they loved her. She retired. Culetta Burdette became the vineyard manager and has been here for 30 plus years. She's quiet but she knows what she's doing. We use a local force, for a week of work you get pay plus a bottle of wine. Kids and grandkids are now working here."

Over my many visits to Markko, I spoke with Culetta Burdette (see Picture 10) a few times but she is very reserved and a lady of few words. Culetta's strengths, which make her an excellent vineyard manager, are her ability to listen, digest the information and communicate clearly to Arnie and the crew. Arnie obviously has trust in Culetta to manage the crew but I'm not sure he always comes across that way. Arnie is a bit of a micro-manager but then again I've never really met a winemaker who isn't. During one visit in June of 2016, when I could actually get a few minutes from Culetta's busy day, I wanted to get some background on her but she wanted to talk about Linda Frisbie. Culetta spoke about Linda and said "Linda taught me a lot about the vineyard, frankly everything. She learned what she knew from Arnie and what she learned over the years and in her own tough but loving way she taught me. I guess I've worked at Markko for about 30 years, and I think my title is the Crew Chief." Culetta is not interested in telling you her story, and you have to respect that.

Picture 10: Culetta Burdette during Pinot Noir bottle labeling
– Photograph by Clifford Annis, Jr.

When talking about the Markko crew, I would be remiss if I didn't talk about Ted Burdette (see Picture 11). Ted is the Vineyard Maintenance Manager and is the brother in-law to Culetta Burdette. Ted is a hard worker who I truly believe does almost every maintenance job at the winery. There's not a job Ted won't do; he is a true cellar rat. He will crawl under and climb on anything to get the job done and done right. Ted might be short in stature but the man is strong as an ox. Ted is another one who does not like to talk about himself and I never could persuade him to. He affectionately calls Arnie "the old man" and he is a bottom line kind a guy. He tells you like it is and most of time in "colorful" language with a sprinkle of humor added in.

*Picture 11: Ted Burdette working on pressing grapes
– Photograph by Clifford Annis, Jr.*

To give you a glimpse of Ted's humor and the fun the crew has, I'll relay an incident from a visit to Markko on November 2, 2016. This was the day Markko was pressing the recently picked Cabernet Sauvignon grapes. Culetta and Nancy Allen (retired nurse and part of the crew; Picture 12), were using five gallon buckets to scoop the grapes out of the bins and transfer them to the press. Ted was monitoring the press and pumping the pressed juice into a stainless steel holding tank with Arnie watching like a hawk. The leftover pressed grape skins dropped into boxes below the press to be collected and sent to Mayfield Creamery to be used to make Markko Gouda. Bucket after bucket was dumped into the press and the bins with the pressed grapes had

33

a wonderful aroma. By the end of the back breaking job, the ladies hands and shirts were a dark purple color and frankly looked like they had just come from a paint ball battle. Ted turned to me and said "They're ready for their prom dates now."

Picture 12: Nancy Allen (left) and Culetta Burdette (right) working on pressing Cabernet grapes – Photograph by Clifford Annis, Jr.

As the pressing continued, Ted walked over to me and said "The grapes are collected in the field and de-stemmed and added to the bins to settle. Then, the grapes are stomped to add oxygen and you keep stomping to get the sugars and the natural yeast going. The alcohol comes up and you get a buzz". The stomped grapes are referred to as grape slurry. The pressing is a slow process to say the least. I was asking Arnie about the pressing process and how it works, when all of the sudden Arnie said with a gasp, "Oh shit, the compressor needs to be on". The crew burst out laughing. Ted had a big old grin on his face and didn't say a word. Ted called me over by the press at one point and said "It's a lot of work but four years later it is worth it". He's not kidding about that.

Just about that time, Arnie yelled out to Ted, remember it was very noisy with the grape press operating, "I need the empty grape bin moved so I can get in the tank." Ted barked to Arnie "If you move your skinny butt out of the way, I will move it. If I need your help I will call." The crew let out a hearty laugh and then went straight back to work. The tank that had been holding the grapes to allow initial fermentation needed to be empty and has no valve at the bottom. Arnie said the rest needed to be emptied by hand. Ted said "Okay, I will jump in there, scoop up the rest and I won't do a number one while I'm in there." Arnie laughed and decided he would get in the tank himself. Arnie stripped down to his skivvies, at 85 years old, climbed in the tank with a 5 gallon bucket and scooped out the reminder of the grape slurry (see Picture 13 below). There is no rest for the weary during the harvest at Markko.

Picture 13: Arnie Esterer in the grape holding tank
– Photograph by Clifford Annis, Jr.

During a visit with Arnie back on October 17, 2017, Arnie decided we needed to pay a visit to the Cabernet Sauvignon vineyard. The Cabernet vineyard is on the south side of Interstate 90, and consists of twenty rows of Cabernet Sauvignon, with Merlot and Chambourcin mixed in. As were walking out into vines, Arnie said "Cab vineyard buds out later and is more resistant to frost. It is warmer here and 50 feet higher in evaluation versus the Riesling. It is all tiled. We put tile down almost four feet for drainage. The roots don't like too much water, they don't like wet feet. Tile helps drain off the water from the roots. We ploughed it 30 inches deep above the tile." There is a farm across the road owned by the son of Arnie's former crew chief. Her name was Lucile Kelly. Arnie said "We called her loose wheel. She could out pick anybody and would yell at the other pickers. She would say "I know how to tie grapes". She showed me all of the little tricks the Concord growers had; how you could be more efficient. She had her sisters out here. She was president of TOPS (Take Off Pounds Sensibly). It was a ladies group. She and her sisters and all her friends at TOPS would come out and pick grapes. They would work in the vineyard and do tying. She knew how to do all the jobs in the vineyard, and she was a good leader of people. She died back in the 1990's, in 1992 or 1993 I think. I had to find a new leader. I looked around. I had this lady named Maryellen Burdette, so, I made her boss one day. The crew came in at the end of the day and said if she's boss tomorrow we're out of here. So, I kept looking and looking. Everyone would say Aunt Culetta said this or that. Culetta had been here for 5 years, so I made her the boss and she is still here. Culetta is real quiet and doesn't cause any trouble. Culetta lost her husband a couple of years ago. She has two good boys and a grandson. Now her great grandchildren are working here." Arnie continues "The interesting guy who is back is Chris Jarvey, who is Linda's grandson. He came in and said I want to work for Markko Vineyard. He's in the Marine Corp. reserves. Chris is good kid. We just have multiple generations working here and I hope it continues long after I'm gone."

In the more than 50 years of Markko Vineyard, many have contributed to the winery's success. There have been many crews over the years and, unfortunately, they all can't be mentioned here (see Pictures 14 – 18). Markko is an estate winery, with vineyards, winemaking, bottling, labeling and distribution all happening on 100+ acres in Conneaut, Ohio. As Arnie always tells me "many hands make light work" and it takes two families, Arnie's God given family and the wine family, to make the wines of Markko Vineyard. I think it was said best in one of the older issues of Markko's *Gadding Vine* (No. 12, Fall 1983)[16], when they were talking about the 1983 harvest and closed with the following:

> "The story of this year's harvest isn't complete without giv-
> ing credit to the valuable picking crew who are part of the
> Markko family: Linda Frisbie, Lucille Kelly (captain), Karen
> Christensen, Dave, Bernie, Carmeena, Jeff, Mary Ann,
> Christine, Ed, Christine and Dennis Frisbie, Terri, Rachael
> and Bob. This cheerful, hardy group is the real backbone of
> Markko. Thanks for the long hours and hard work." [16]

Picture 14: The Markko Crew circa 2015 (Linda Frisbie is first row center;

Arnie first row far right)

Picture 15: Markko Crew in the field July 2018 (Ted Burnette on the tractor; Culetta Burnette third from the right) - Photography courtesy of Jim Messenheimer

Picture 16: The Markko Crew circa 2016

(Arnie is on the left in the front row)

Picture 17: Arnie Esterer in the vineyard (circa 2014)

Picture 18: One of the very first Markko Crews (date unknown)
– Photography courtesy of Jim Messenheimer

CHAPTER **3**

Tim Hubbard and Linda Frisbie – Two Thirds of Genius

Tim Hubbard (May 29, 1923 – January 14, 2000)

Picture 19: Drawing of Tim Hubbard by Martta Tuomloa (date unknown) – Drawing courtesy of Martta Tuomloa

IT CAN'T BE overstated that Markko Vineyard may not have come to pass if it wasn't for Arnie's 32 year partnership and friendship with the late Tim Hubbard (see Picture 19). Arnie considered Tim more than just a partner; he was a like the older brother Arnie never had. During the numerous visits with Arnie, when we talked about Tim Hubbard, Arnie always stopped and got a bit teary eyed.

On June 8, 2016, Arnie and I sat down and had one of our first discussions about Tim Hubbard. Arnie met Tim at the art center in Ashtabula which Katy had helped start. Tim died of Mesothelioma on January 14, 2000. He worked with chlorine gas and salts and had been exposed to asbestos when he was younger. He was a corporal in the Army during World War II and fought in France. Tim told Arnie he always felt lucky that he was able to come back alive. He never married until he was 58 years old. Arne had met Cissy Cochran at a wine tasting event at the Butler Wick Museum in Youngstown, Ohio where she was the director. After the event, Arnie went out to Charlie's Crab restaurant and ran into Cissy again. She was recently divorced and Arnie being married said, "You need to meet my partner Tim". When Arnie returned from the function, he told Tim about Cissy. The two met and the rest is history. Arnie said, "I remember Tim was all excited about getting married. It was in 1980. Cissy and Tim had two kids, Polly and Luke, and a step daughter Elizabeth from Cissy's previous marriage. Tim was always willing to support a good cause. He promoted the Underground Railroad in the area and he started the Hubbard House museum as well as the Marine Museum, both located in Ashtabula. Tim often walked up and down the street picking up trash; He didn't like that we used paper towels…he was a conservationist and a very generous man. Tim donated a couple hundred acres of land to the Cleveland Natural History Museum and was on the Board of Directors of Erie Insurance Company. Tim kept working at the vineyard, even when he was dying." Arnie showed me the newspaper clippings on Tim's death. The paper had listed him as Sam Hubbard. Arnie said "Well, that was an oops!" Arnie chuckled and said "Tim was fired as a Sunday school teacher. He was Episcopalian and he didn't teach the way they wanted him to. He was very liberal."

During another visit on July 28, 2016, Arnie spoke of Tim without me even prompting him to. Arnie said "Tim was good to everyone. We started the partnership in 1968 and stayed partners until he died. Tim was a quiet guy and very humble. Day to day, I ran the winery and Tim was the financial backer. Tim liked to preserve old houses. Trent and Norma Bobbitt, who were active in home restoration, were good friends of his and Tim helped them restore the Sandisfield House. We did tastings there for years. At the Sandisfield tastings, the Trents would dress up as old settlers from the area. Tim liked to preserve the history of Ashtabula County and saw the vineyard as a new industry that would fit in with the preservation of the area." Arnie continued "Tim drank wine and was a man about town. Tim would take wine over to the Rabbit Run Theater in Madison and before the show or during intermission, he would pour wine. He would go to Youngstown and pour wine, and he would even take wine to the Board Meetings of the Erie Insurance Company. In other words, Tim would always take wine with him wherever he went as he knew we could not solely rely on friends to be our customers. Tim was supportive of the idea I had that vinifera grapes could be grown in this region and would have a long-term future because of the lake. We saw the future in this region as Dr. Frank saw it in New York. Tim and I had the same vision for the vineyard which made our partnership work. Whenever we needed a couple thousand dollars to do something, like buy tanks or barrels, he would come up with the money. Tim believed in Markko from the first day until his last."

When Tim was diagnosed with Mesothelioma, he received a substantial financial settlement. During a dinner back in August 2018 with Arnie, his son David and old friend Jerry Danalchak, Arnie recalled Tim being generous to the end. Arnie said "Tim was in his final hours of life in hospice and he said he wanted to do something for Linda. Linda had bought a house with six acres of land and had about $20,000 left on the mortgage. Tim wanted to pay off the house so he wrote a check right then and there." Arnie continued "The hospice guy, that was you Jerry, was there along with Cissy and me. My son David had come home so I told Tim I had to make a quick trip home to see him and Tim said okay. As I was going out the door he sat up in bed and screamed "GOOD BYE!" I thought Jesus, that was random, and that is the last thing I remember about him. Those were his last words to me. I got the call to hurry back, but I was dragging my feet as I hate to see people die. By the time I got back he was gone." David Esterer had gone back with Arnie to see Tim and remembered walking in and hearing Cissy say "Well it's been quite a production tonight". Jerry added "That was one of the most unique deaths I've ever seen because Tim said goodbye and that was it." Arnie lifted his wine glass and said "Tim was like that, he was very generous. Let's drink to Linda and Tim! Cheers!"

I asked Arnie what he would most want people to remember about Tim Hubbard. Arnie thought for a minute and said "He was very humble. He could accept almost anything, was very quiet and would do anything for the winery."

Just as Arnie finished reminiscing about Tim, Arnie said "Oh, I have to tell this Tim story. Tim had box at the Cleveland Orchestra. The box held eight seats and Tim would always put a party together every Friday night during the season. We would have dinner at *Isabella's*, where they carried Markko wines. Tim would invite eight people who would sit in the box but he would go into the restroom, lay down in the back, and go to sleep. Tim was promoting the Orchestra and filling up the box. That was Tim, always thinking of others."

In Markko's newsletter *The Gadding Vine* (No. 47)[17] from the summer 1980 edition, Arnie wrote the following heart felt tribute to Tim:

"**TIM HUBBARD**: As many of you already know, Tim

Hubbard died on January 14, 2000. In addition to being a partner, Tim was like an older brother. We founded Markko Vineyard in 1968. In the early days we traveled together to Hammondsport, New York to graft vines with Dr. Frank and to learn how to grow vinifera vines. From there we planted the first and second vineyard together. The design and construction of the winery was next. Tim was always an important part of Markko whether he was creating ideas that answered vineyard problems or pouring wines at events like Rabbit Run Theater or Cleveland Symphony Development dinners. For his friends, he carried wine, cider, a loaf of bread, apples or blueberries to share. He met Cissy Cochran at a wine function at the Butler Wick Museum in Youngstown. They courted, married and raised a family: Elizabeth, Polly and Luke. (Tim and Cissy shared a passion for the arts and a strong interest in history. Both families had histories of involvement with the Underground Railroad. The William Hubbard House, now the Hubbard House Underground RR Museum, was an integral part of the escape route from the South to Canada.)

Thanks to all of you for the sympathy and support through all of Tim's trials. He kept active and engaged in all his activities right to the very last day. He and his family gained strength from your concern and good wishes. Those here at the Vineyard feel the loss more than words can express. We see the same future that he saw and shared with enthusiasm. The goal now is to hold to the course and build on the ideals he nurtured over the last thirty-two years. As he requested we "shed no tears" and remember that "many hands make light work."[17]

Linda G. Frisbie (June 4, 1940 – July 12, 2015)

*Pictures 20 & 21: Linda Frisbie at her post in the Markko tasting room –
Picture 21 courtesy of the family of Linda Frisbie*

Without a doubt, Linda Frisbie was a very important part of the success of Markko Vineyard and she worked alongside Arnie for 40 years. Whether she was out in the fields tending to her beloved Cabernet vines, standing behind the tasting counter ready to pour for a customer (see Pictures 20 and 21), watching over the crew, arguing with Arnie over some new experimental idea he had or tending to a barrel of Muscat in the wine cellar, Linda was always present. The story of Linda is the story of a hard working mother who loved Markko like her child and fiercely protected it. The character she possessed, the sacrifices she made to make Markko wines the best they could be and her unending loyalty to Markko and Arnie should leave no doubt as to who this lady was and why the greater Markko family will never forget the impact she had on Markko Vineyard.

My first interview with Arnie occurred on August 31, 2015; Linda's death on July 12th, 2015, of a heart attack was still fresh in Arnie's mind. As I had only met Linda once in April at Founder's Day, which happened to be the last day she worked at Markko, Arnie was keen on wanting to talk about her. Arnie poured us a glass of 2010 Cabernet Sauvignon which was fitting as this was the wine she spent much of her time tending to. He recalled "Linda showed up here in 1975 and wanted to pick grapes. She was in her truck and had a one year old baby next to her and asked "you need any help?" I said sure, you can come and pick grapes tomorrow and she started the next day. Linda enjoyed working with the grapes in the vineyard. She learned to prune the vines and took a particular interest in red grapes, especially Cab. She wasn't afraid to get on her hands and knees and learned to crop the grapes. When I wasn't there, she'd tell the crew how much crop to take off to make them ripen. She was always reading wine magazines and would see an article and say hey Arnie read this. We should be doing this. She always was eager to learn. Linda was physically strong and could lift a barrel on her own. We would taste sixty barrels of Chardonnay although you only need 10 for the bottling. Linda and I would go down in the cellar and taste the barrels; she took notes. She could detect little nuances. She had a lot of talent and a super palate which she developed slowly over time." Arnie surprised me when he said "I bet you didn't know she never drank wine…always drank Pepsi. She would taste the wine and spit it out. She had great ability to taste…great palate but didn't know it. She was in AA (Alcoholics Anonymous) for 40 years."

Linda had a hard life and tragedy always seem to follow her. Arnie recalled "One day I came back to the vineyard and saw smoke coming from the direction of Linda's house. I ran down there and there was Linda all dressed up, she had just gotten home and the house was totally in a blaze and gutted. Her dogs were killed. The owner of the house Linda was renting from didn't like her so he set the house on fire while she was out. The guy wouldn't look at me; he thought I was an agent of the Devil because I was making wine. She had a real hard life."

The worst pain any parent can have is losing a child. Linda had to endure this in her life when her son Denis Frisbie died at the age of 26. Arnie recalled that horrible day as one he would never forget. "It was February 2001. There was big smoke up on the hill. Chris, Linda's daughter was here at the winery. We got up to Linda's house, the one Tim Hubbard had paid off the mortgage on, and the fire department was on the job. The neighbor had called and they were treating it like a garage fire. We said there are two people in there but Denis and his girlfriend, Melissa Wassie, were killed in the fire. Denis's death was tough on Linda and me. She had a lot of tragedy in her life."

Arnie continued "Denis used to work here. He was the baby in Linda's truck when she showed up here in 1975. He grew up here at Markko and worked odd jobs here after school. Unfortunately, he got into drugs and stopped coming around. He was arrested in Erie and I posted a $5,000 bond and got him out. He did pay me back but Linda was pissed and said to leave him in jail. Denis came to me one day when I was out in the vineyard. He was all dressed up in clean clothes with his hair combed and we had a talk. I asked him to come and live with me but he said no. He went back to his girlfriend and ended up back on drugs. Later, he came to me one day and said he couldn't understand how I could put up with all the things he did. I said I tried to help and you can always count on me. After her son died in the fire, Linda wouldn't live in the house anymore. She wouldn't touch the house but she wouldn't let anyone else have it either. Her kids couldn't have it; her grandkids couldn't have it. She moved out and that was that."

During Founder's Day 2016, I had an opportunity to speak with many of Markko's loyal customers about Linda. What seems to be the common theme regarding Linda can best be expressed by the words of Tom and Joyce Kmiecik. Tom and Joyce have been friends of Markko Vineyard for many years. When I asked them to sum up Linda in a few thoughts, Tom and Joyce spoke highly of her devotion to Arnie, Markko and the quality and integrity of Markko wines. Tom said "the first day I met Linda I felt like I was back in Sunday school and the nun was going to whack my hands with the ruler. Once you got to know her, she was a very nice person; you just needed to crack the shell. You had to get within her small inner circle."

Speaking of the inner circle, during a visit to Markko in June of 2016, I was finally able to briefly break into the inner circle and speak with Culetta Burdette. Culetta is basically the person who has tried to fill Linda's shoes, which isn't an easy job. I knew I wasn't going to get another shot at this, so I asked her point blank what she would like people to know about Linda. Culetta was quiet for a few minutes and then said, "She was a great teacher but tough and you needed to stay on her good side. She was one of a kind. She could be tough but taught us a lot and knew a tremendous amount about the vineyard." At that point, Culetta excused herself and headed out to the vineyard, where I believe is truly one of her favorite places to be. The inner circle had been breached but never again.

While visiting Arnie in October 2017, Arnie recalled Linda's love for her family and had a story he wanted in the book. We sat down in the tasting room with our ever present glass of Cabernet, the wine of choice when Linda's name came up. Arnie smiled, took a sip and said "Every Sunday, Linda would go out with her sister, mother and father to a restaurant over in Painesville for brunch. They would spend all Sunday morning there. She always wanted $200 in cash on pay day, and one bill had to be a $50. She would buy lunch for everyone and would give the $50 to her father, Donald. She never wanted to go to a bank, so I would deposit the rest of pay for her. Founder's Day 2015 was the last day she worked. She had a heart attack after that. She was tough, very honest and loving. If I had to sum it up, it was tough love."

I finally had a chance to speak with the busy Greg Johns, the retired Director of the Ohio State University Grape Research Center, back on October 17, 2017. Greg conveyed a story he told at Linda's funeral. "Linda was responsible for the good Cabs at Markko. Arnie would go out to the island in Canada every year, every summer for 4 or 5 or 6 days. As soon as Linda saw the tail lights disappear down the driveway, she would go out into the Cab vineyard and start thinning the crops. Arnie wouldn't know that she did it. She took the grapes and put them in her trunk in boxes and she'd drive down the road and dump them in the ditch so when he'd get back he would be none the wiser. Honestly, Arnie's trips to Canada are probably the reason why the Cabs have been so great here. The Cabs here are equal to or better than the Cabs in southern Ohio and they are doing a wonderful job with Cabs in southern Ohio."

I had a second chance to speak with Greg Johns in August of 2018 after Arnie had called him to arrange our get together. I asked Greg, who currently owns a vineyard over in Madison, to share what he would want the readers to know about Linda. Greg nodded his head and said "Linda had a super palate and she made Markko wines what they are. She kept them from making mistakes. She learned everything about winemaking (Enology) and grape growing (viticulture) right here. She taught herself a lot and read a lot about wine. We talked a lot about the vineyard, the viticulture of how the vines grow and she saw all that. She would pick the brains of all the winemakers who visited...constant was her willingness to learn and her ability and memory, were fabulous. Whenever you asked for anything, she knew where it was and she owned it."

I could tell Greg wasn't finished and he had something on his mind. I asked him to share, from his perspective, who Linda Frisbie was and what he believes is her legacy. Greg paused for a moment and said, "The big thing was she was under-appreciated for a lot of years. Customers did not know how to take her because she was kind of gruff. She would approach you with her gray hair (blonde when she was younger) tied back, and with long finger nails. She'd be smoking her cigarette and some people did not know how to take her. They thought she was a little bit stand-offish but really she was letting the customer make their own decisions. When she got a feel for what the customer liked, she would offer a certain vintage whether it was a new one or an old one. She never pushed anything on them and I think Arnie liked that about her. She would sit back behind the counter in the high chair and let them do their tasting. She was there when they needed her, but otherwise she didn't get in their face like many pourers at other vineyard tasting rooms. That's part of the feeling of Markko and part of the way it's been run. The customer will decide which wines they like the best and you don't have to push them. You can make them aware of certain wines but don't push. She was really good in the tasting room. She came to work at the vineyard green as grass just as I did, but she learned from planting baby grapes to the point she knew everything about pruning and tying, removing leaves and adjusting crops and her knowledge extended into the cellar and to her palate. She developed a very good palate unfortunately not too many people realized that. I don't think even Arnie realized what a great palate Linda had until after she was gone. Even though it's little old Linda in the corner and you could take her advice or leave it, she was usually right about what to blend, what not to blend, if something had residual sugar or not. She may have not had the fancy words to describe what she was tasting but she knew what she was talking about. She knew when to tell Arnie "Don't blend those two barrels, you'll ruin them." She was kind of gruff that way. She said that to me before…"don't do that you'll ruin it." You just had to learn that was Linda's personality. You could have tons of fun with her and she would have tons of fun right back with you. We all miss Linda. She was here every day come hell or high water; it didn't matter if it was her birthday. If something was going on here Christmas Day she would be here. Even when she announced her retirement at one of the events here, the next day she was back again and stayed for the next couple of years. She was supposed to retire but she never did. Her retirement was when she died. Linda and I were very close friends and we always would go out to dinner together with her son. Linda would take her father out to dinner and she would take her kids out to dinner all the time. I miss her."

I have visited Marrko many times over the past four years and I can't think of a single time Linda's name didn't come up. Arnie told me many times that Markko's success was due in a large part to Linda. As stated previously, Markko Vineyard was Linda's life and Arnie never recalled a day that Linda wasn't there. She was truly dedicated until the end.

After Linda passed away, Arnie sat down and wrote a wonderful loving poem in memory of his dear friend. If you knew nothing of Linda and this was the first thing you read about her, you would walk away saying I wish I had known her. Cheers to you Linda; rest in heavenly peace.

In Memory of Linda Frisbie
(June 4, 1940 to July 12, 2015)

She came in a pickup
with a one-year-old on the front seat
"Do you need help?"
"Sure. Come pick grapes tomorrow."

She did – long finger nails and all,
a gun and knife under the seat.
Her chicken cooked in foil
five miles on the exhaust manifold.

For Lucille they picked vines,
 then loaded and pressed boxes
of whole bunches into juice
-must for fermenting barrels

In deep blurring snow she pruned
back to back with Bernie
their mesh steel gloves-on
tied to snapping pneumatic sheers.

Each missing vine she knew
called for replacement.
So winter grafting, a nursery
with spring replanting followed.

Cabernet being last,
coldest and a challenge to ripen,
became her focus in the vineyard
with Ali's guide to winemaking.

Always tireless on her knees
the Cabs' got special care.
Questioning everything!
she held total control of red grapes

Presses held secrets only she found
each load tucked boxes to tanks.
But cold crushed Reds needed
her special warming touch to start

From Helene, vineyard and wine,
she saw, became one.
Her fussy pallet could nose-out a barrel,
then marry a 10-batch prize winner.

Customers sometimes wondered
then loved her for truth, trust,
honest compassionate friendship,
and outstanding memory of them.

Culetta and crew developed a respect
for her strong views and methods.
She saved everything but knew where it was.
Daily her chimney smoke signaled warmth to all

With Gregg, Mario and friends,
she learned and shared her help, advice and feelings.
Students got the benefit of many
practical and studied years.

Linda gave her life to Markko Vineyard.
She recorded each vine, and every step
from barrel to bottle to customer –
a living legacy in a remarkable life work.

But last and most important of all
everyone in family stayed in her heart.
Daily meals together, then Sunday Brunch
Linda, all past and future generations lovingly say, "Well
Done"

By Arnie W. Esterer, July 16, 2015

Doug Moorhead, Bill Konnerth, Brother David Petry, Allen Holmes, Leon Adams and Joe Cooper

AS ARNIE HAS reminded me many times, Markko's success would not have been possible without the guidance, helping hands and coaching from many wine pioneers and passionate supporters in and around the wine industry. Over the times Arnie and I have spent together, I've learned there were a few key individuals that impacted Arnie and Markko the most. Some of these include Doug Moorhead and Bill Konnerth of Presque Isle Wine Cellars, famous Cleveland attorney, Allen Holmes, world renowned wine writer, Leon Adams, Benedictine Monk, Brother David Petry and former President of The International Wine and Food Society, Joe Cooper. It is only fitting that a chapter be devoted to their contributions.

Doug Moorhead and William (Bill) Konnerth (1911-2005) – Presque Isle Wine Cellars

From the first day I met Arnie and we discussed the idea of a book about him and Markko, the names of Doug Moorhead (see Picture 22) and Bill Konnerth were first on Arnie's list of those who impacted him the most, Dr. Frank notwithstanding. Arnie said "You should talk to Doug Moorhead. The late Bill Konnerth was a partner of Doug's when they founded Prescott Isle Wine Cellars. That's how this whole industry grew up around here. They lead me to Dr. Frank because Doug was a cooperator of his." Arnie continued "I got started with Doug Moorhead. Doug and Bill were the first to introduce vinifera around here in 1963-1964. He was one of the guys because his father was President of Welches. Doug was stationed in Germany while in the Army. When he came back from Europe, he said you know wine is a big thing over there. We are growing grapes so why the hell aren't we doing something with wine?"

To understand the influence Doug and Bill had on Arnie, it is important to know a little bit about who they are and why Arnie considered them the pioneers of vinifera grape growing in Pennsylvania and the Lake Erie region. Doug was the first in that area to plant vinifera around 1959. Doug Moorhead and Bill Konnerth started Presque Isle Wine Cellars in 1964 to supply grapes and winemaking equipment to the local amateur winemakers in the region. According to the Presque Isle Wine Cellars website, in September 1969, the winery operations commenced after the State of Pennsylvania passed the Limited Winery Act of 1968.[18]

DOUG MOORHEAD, BILL KONNERTH, BROTHER DAVID
PETRY, ALLEN HOLMES, LEON ADAMS AND JOE COOPER

Picture 22: Doug Moorhead, co-founders of Presque Isle Wine Cellars –
Doug's picture courtesy of Presque Isle Wine Cellars website[18]
(Marlene Moorhead)

I had plans to meet with Doug Moorhead in the November 2018
timeframe to learn more about him and Bill. I wanted to know about
Dr. Frank's impact on Doug and to discuss Arnie's contribution to the
Ohio wine industry but that wasn't to be. Unfortunately, Doug had
a severe stroke at the end of June 2018. Arnie and I spoke with his
wife, Marlene, by phone on October 18th, and Marlene said "This one
is really bad. He was in the hospital in rehabilitation and has been
released from all that. He's at home but not making much progress
so it is sad, sad, sad." Marlene expanded "He has had friends in to
see him and he talks a lot but it's not connected to reality. Every once
in a while he connects and it's astounding when he does. He doesn't
know people though. He really doesn't even know our son Erik. It is a
mysterious thing because some things he knows but not everything."
Marlene referred me to the winery's website where I could learn more
about Doug and Bill.

As documented on the Presque Isle Wine Cellars website[18] and per Marlene's recommendation, here is the background on Doug Moorhead, followed by Bill Konnerth.

"**Doug Moorhead** grew up on a fruit farm in Harborcreek Township in Erie County, PA, and at 80 still farms on his 170 acre family-owned vineyard, in addition to his activities with Presque Isle Wine Cellars. He graduated from Penn State in 1956 with a degree in Pomology. To help his family get by during the Great Depression, Doug's father, Douglas McCord Moorhead, had a side business brokering what few wine varieties there were in the area with several small ethnic wineries in or near Cleveland, Ohio and with Gold Seal Vineyards and Widmer Vineyards in the Finger Lakes Region. He was also very active in cooperatives in the Lake Erie area and was President of National Grape Cooperative when it was able to purchase Welch Foods and vastly improve the economic prospects of Concord growers. He was later President of Welch Foods in the late 1950's. Douglas P Moorhead grew up in that environment and became interested in the economics of growing wine grapes to replace the acreage of other fruits such as sweet and sour cherries, peaches, plums and apples, which had become less and less profitable in the Lake Erie area. Doug had also experimented with nearly 200 French Hybrid varieties and had introduced the growing of European grapes (Vitis vinifera) into the Lake Erie area in the late 1950's. One of his main interests has been to produce quality wines from traditional European grapes grown in Pennsylvania, a goal which several other wineries in the state are now also accomplishing."[18]

"Doug was the first chairman of a State Grape Marketing Council, which developed the legislative proposal that became the Pennsylvania Limited Winery Act in 1968. He was a long time director and a past president of The Pennsylvania Wine Association, was a long time director in the National Grape Cooperative, which owns Welch Foods, and was an adjunct professor in the culinary department at Mercyhurst College in North East, PA. He is currently a director of

Wine America and The Pennsylvania Grape Marketing Board. He is
also the Vice President of Presque Isle Wine Cellars."

"In recognition of his accomplishments and contributions to the industry, in 2013 Doug became only the second person to be honored
by the Pennsylvania Wine Association with a Lifetime Achievement
Award. Doug is a proud Penn Stater and distinguished alum."

"**Bill Konnerth** grew up in Erie, PA, and was a graduate of The
University of Pittsburgh. He spent some time on the roads since jobs
were not readily available when he graduated. He had a varied working background including chief electrician at a US Steel Coal Mine
and later owning a cabinet making shop in Erie that specialized in
restoring antiques that had suffered damage. He had relatives who
had operated wineries in Erie before Prohibition which sparked his
interest in wine. The cabinet making shop began when he had arranged to purchase a country weekly newspaper in Hammondsport,
NY, only to have the owner renege on the sale at the time of closing.
He was the original winemaker and retired from Presque Isle Wine
Cellars in 1975. He spent his remaining years indulging his very active curiosity and becoming a notable amateur videographer. At age
94 was still writing a treatise on the economic effects of free trade,
which he had come to think of as being a very bad thing for the USA.
Bill died in 2005 at age 95. He was the last surviving vice president of
the group headed by Dr. Konstantin Frank and Albert W. Laubengayer
who started the American Wine Society."[18]

The opportunity to speak with Doug Moorhead was gone. However,
there was one saving grace. I attended the American Wine Society's
50th Annual meeting at Pocono Manor, Pennsylvania on November 2
– 4, 2017. One of the key reasons I attended was because some of
Dr. Konstantin Frank's former cooperators were doing a special session
entitled "Dr. Konstantin's "Co-Operators" and Friends – Historic Tales/
Memories of Dr. Frank" in celebration of the 50th anniversary of the first

American Wine Society (AWS) meeting which was organized by Dr. Konstantin Frank himself. That first meeting took place in Western New York at the vineyard of Dr. Frank on Keuka Lake near Hammondsport on October 7, 1967.[19] As luck would have it, one of the former Dr. Frank cooperators scheduled to speak at this special session was Doug Moorhead. As always, I took my trusty recorder and taped the entire session with the permission of the AWS. They wanted a copy of the recording because they hadn't thought to record it themselves. When it came time for Doug to speak, Arnie, who was on the distinguished panel of former cooperators, looked over at me and mouthed "Get all of this...this is why Doug was so important to Markko." Instead of giving you a "Cliff notes" version (you can smile or snicker), here are Doug's exact words transcribed from my recording:

Doug Moorhead own words: "I'm as old as dirt but that epitaph was given to me 17 years ago and I'm still here. I met Dr. Frank...we made the obligatory visit to Gold Seal and we were escorted to his work shop which had no windows in it and there were no plants growing in there. We went in and he was very cordial and gave us a lot of information and then he started pouring samples. My younger brother was a senior in high school or a freshman in college and hadn't had much chance to drink before that and after we had 3 nice big samples, I went over and talked to him and said look you haven't had a lot of experience on this and I will try to help you when you get as far as you want on a glass I'll finish it off. Three samples later I cut him loose and said you're on your own." (Crowd laughs) And the three of us very mellow went down the hill to Bath and had dinner and had a wonderful day and I was able to get grafted roots the next spring so we planted our first vinifera's in 1959 and went along very well for a while but I had an experience come up. Dr. Frank told me there were a couple of researchers in Germany and I think John Stavisky is going to talk more about that Hanz Brighter and

Elizabeth Wolfe and they came out with a research finding that when chickens drank wine from hybrids or native grapes their feathers were going to have funny molts on them, legs were deformed and one shouldn't drink hybrid wines. Then Dr. Frank came to me and said I needed to tear out all those hybrids and I spent a few years trying to get those planted and I didn't buy into the research and it turned out to be many years later that it was other reasons of toxicity that gave the chickens trouble. But Dr. Frank said I won't sell you anymore vinifera grafts if you don't tear them out (hybrids). But he went to my then partner and found out what he wanted then we ended up getting all of them. I paid the check with my name on them and Dr. Frank always cashed them. (Crowd laughs) But those of my generation owe a grant debt to Dr. Frank. He gave us some of the things that made it easier for us to grow in our climate and I'm still at it some 60 years later." (Crowd stands and applauds) [20]

The importance of Doug Moorhead to Markko can't be emphasized enough. During the phone conversation Arnie and I had with Marlene Moorhead back in October 2018, I mentioned that Arnie had told me numerous times about Doug being very influential in Arnie's connection with Dr. Frank. Marlene said, "Right, I'm trying to remember. Doug was involved with his father, and that was probably how it started. Doug's father was good friends with Charles Fournier, who was associated with Gold Seal Winery. Doug and his father delivered grapes to Great Western and Gold Seal which were separate wineries at that time. Gold Seal, Great Western, Taylor and Widmer, they delivered grapes to all of those wineries and that would have been in the late 1950's and maybe all through the 50's. That would have been how Doug met Dr. Frank who was working at Gold Seal for Charles Fournier at that time. Doug was probably the first person outside of the Finger Lakes to get involved with Dr. Frank." Arnie said, "Doug was the one who brought vinifera to Lake Erie" and Marlene replied,

"Yep, that is correct but you, Arnie, brought and proved vinifera could work in northeastern Ohio. It was you Arnie."

Arnie and Doug have been good friends for over 54 years, so the phone call with Marlene was very emotional. Arnie was thinking of his old friend as well as his own mortality and he turned to me and said "Doug, what a shame...good man...sad day today".

Brother David Petry, Monk of Saint Meinrad Archabbey (November 6, 1931 – November 14, 1985)

Brother David Petry was a Monk of Saint Meinrad Archabbey, Indiana and a cooperator of Dr. Frank. Arnie recalled how he met Brother David during one of our talks back in April 2018. Arnie said, "1974 was the first time I went down to the Abby. I can't remember exactly when Brother David started with Dr. Frank, but he was a cooperator of his. Brother David was the winemaker at the Abbey where they also had Dr. Frank's wine. Dr. Frank provided them with sacramental wine. Brother David decided to go visit Dr. Frank and he stayed for a whole year. He went there and worked for Dr. Frank and learned the whole cycle of pruning, harvesting, everything. He did whatever Dr. Frank wanted him to do. He would come to work each day and work eight hours or more. Dr. Frank got him started and sent him back with a whole bunch of vinifera and root stock and everything else. I met Brother David when he attended the Ohio Wine Grape conferences. In 1983 when my mother died, he was right there with me. I remember being at the Ohio State Grapevine short course with Bill Worthy, who was the winemaker at the Grand River Vineyard. I said Brother David is coming so let's visit him at the Abbey which was located 10 miles north of the Ohio River. Brother David had a 5,000 gallon winery. The monks didn't have a license but they were making wine. They had been making wine with Concord grapes and now Brother David was going to use Dr. Frank's vinifera. We toured the place and then it was time for vespers. They had a Gregorian chant book, so when the monks all sang, we sang along with them. It was a feast day and they invited us to stay for dinner. Usually the monks aren't permitted to talk during meals but as this was a feast day, they were allowed. There were 160 monks and they were all sitting around talking and having a good time. After dinner, we toured the School of Theology and by then it was like 10 o'clock at night. Brother David said let me see if I can get you a room but there wasn't a room at the inn. We were not there on a retreat, we were not there on a religious trip, so we had to hop in the car and drive 65 miles to Louisville, KY, just to get a room. That Abbey is out in the middle of nowhere. Later I went back and became an oblate and spent a lot of time there. I worked with Brother David and helped him in the vineyard; helped him with winemaking. It was a beautiful winery and they made 5,000 gallons of wine a year for the Abbey. He ran the vineyard for 10 – 15 years as a hermit. Brother David had a good site and did the right things with it. He died of bladder cancer on November 14, 1985 when he was 55 years old. After Brother David died, Brother Dominic took over but he wasn't really a winemaker. The Abbot, who is the ultimate authority at the Abbey, declared Brother Dominic was drinking too much wine and had to join AA. While I was at the Abbey, at first I was just helping Brother David, but over time we became good friends. The man had the most beautiful penmanship I've ever seen and his writing was poetry. The last I heard from him was a hand written letter dated November 12th, 1985. He died two days later but you wouldn't know it from his letter."

Arnie was right about Brother David's writing, it was beautiful and thoughtful. Below are two excerpts from his last later to Arnie, two days before he lost his battle with cancer.

"It's mid-morning in So. Indiana on a sunny but windy day. I've been sitting here watching the leaves sail past my window. It's not that I haven't anything to do, but sometimes it's good to just sit and watch things happen. Besides, the leaves dance so beautifully – then surely deserve an audience."

"As you know, I stopped in Hammondsport before going on to visit brothers & sisters on Long Island. I knew Dr. Frank had grown feeble with the years, but it was still a little sad to see him almost helpless. But Mama, that strong & wonderful woman, takes good care of him."

Allen C. Holmes
(May 27, 1920 – November 31, 1990)

In the 50 plus years of Markko Vineyard, Arnie told me that no one person has been more influential in putting Markko on the map than the late Allen C. Holmes (see Picture 23 below).

Courtesy of Cleveland Public Library.

Picture 23: Allen C. Holmes
– Picture courtesy of the Cleveland Public Library

Allen C. Holmes had a major impact on the success of Markko Vineyards, not in providing guidance on growing grapes or pruning techniques but, as Arnie says, in marketing this "little guy's Ohio wines", through his world renowned friends and business contacts. Allen, born and raised in Bethel, Ohio, was a nationally recognized attorney who practiced law at the Cleveland firm then known as Jones, Day, Cockley & Reavis, where he went on to become managing partner and was a nationally recognized expert in antitrust law.[21] As Christopher Johnston stated about Allen's practice on the website *http://clevelandartsprize.org/awardees/allen_holmes.html*, "Holmes's vision and commitment helped build his firm into a national organization, which, 25 years after his retirement in 1986, employed more than 2,400 attorneys and maintained offices in 31 cities around the globe, making it one of the world's largest law firms."[21]

Arnie repeatedly told me that Allen was involved in numerous professional, civic, and volunteer organizations. As an example, the local Cleveland magazine *Town & Country* named Holmes the most powerful man in Cleveland in 1981. Arnie told me once "Allen had a passion for the arts and donated his time and money, especially to the Cleveland Institute of Art and the Cleveland Orchestra. But, Allen's greatest passion was for good food and fine wines. Allen was named Chairman of the North American chapter of The International Wine & Food Society (1983-1984)."

During one of my early meetings with Arnie in August of 2015, Allen Holmes was someone he wanted me to talk about. Arnie said, "One of the most important people, the most helpful to Markko Vineyards was Allen C. Holmes. To start this winery I had to go on the road, so I loaded up my truck and I drove around to all the wine stores I could think of. I wanted them to taste my wine. I went into Shaker Square Beverage in Cleveland right on Shaker Square sometime around 1975-1976. Baron von Lüttwitz was the owner; Don't ask me how to spell it, but that was his name. I did a tasting with Baron and he said, oh yeah, great Chardonnay. Very nice; you need to taste this with Allen Holmes. So I looked Allen Holmes up in the phonebook and gave him a call. I said to him I hear you like Chardonnay. I'm a small wine grower over in Conneaut Ohio and I've got some wine. Would you like to taste it? He said sure. Come up to my office in the Union Commerce Building 9th floor in downtown Cleveland. I got off the elevator and there I was at the entrance to Jones, Day, Reavis & Pogue Attorneys at Law, one of the nation's largest law firms. I knocked on the door and said I'd like to see Allen Holmes. I think I had a couple of bottles of wine with me and I turned down this corridor and went down a spiral staircase. I'm talking with Allen Holmes the Managing Partner of Jones, Day, Reavis & Pogue. We introduced ourselves and I said I understand you want to taste wine and he said yeah lets taste some wine. It is 11 o'clock in the morning but he had glasses at hand and we proceeded to taste my wines. Allen then told me he would take two cases and put it in the Union Club. It turned out Allen was a super wine guy and was very knowledgeable about Bordeaux wines. Over the years, he kept tasting and buying Markko wines. Allen came out to Markko in 1981-82. We were in the cellar going through the barrels, and we were tasting the 1980 Chardonnay when he said Arnie take this one and fine it with 3 egg whites but don't filter it. Then, bottle it for me and I said okay. It turned out that was one of the greatest Chardonnay's Markko ever made. We made it in 1980, bottled it in 1981/82 and it was being auctioned in the late 80's. We were getting $100/bottle at auction. Who was there buying? Allen Holmes."

Arnie continued telling me about Allen. "One day Allen said I want to come out and I'm going to bring some friends on a Sunday. He asked if we'd be open and I said yeah I would be at the winery by 12:30. Well, Linda was there but I was late. Allen Holmes was here and he had his two friends and his son with him. I apologized for being late and Allen said "Sit down!" The friends he had with him were Karen

Horn and her husband. Karen was Chairman of the Federal Reserve (Fed) at that time. He was introducing Markko wines to the Chairman of the Fed...unreal."

Arnie stopped and poured us both a glass of Markko Chardonnay and said, "We did his bottling of that Chardonnay. When Allen Holmes was chairman of the North American Committee of the International Wine and Food Society, he invited Markko to provide wines at a luncheon in Bratenhal, which is a suburb of Cleveland on the east side of the lake. At the luncheon there were 4 – 5 tables with 25 or 30 people. I was introduced to many people and ended up sitting next to the owner of the Beverly Hills Wilshire Hotel in California. It was David Ragone. He graduated from the University of Michigan and Allen Holmes went to Michigan as well. I said oh Michigan; I was there from 1950 to 1955 in the Engineering School. Ragone said I was the dean in the 1950's. I asked what he did now and he said I'm President of Case Western Reserve. Allen presented our wines; he wanted to show off the little guys from Ohio and to show what this region could do for people who knew wine. Allen always promoted our region and this young kid (Arnie) to show what we could do. Oh, almost forgot. His son, Peter Holmes, was a reporter, in Washington and ran the National Press Club. Through Peter, Allen arranged a tasting at the Ritz with four or five Ohio wineries represented, Markko being one of them. When Allen died in 1990, we did an Allen Holmes memorial label. We couldn't have done this without him, period."

Allen Holmes was connoisseur of fine wines. He knew the best wines in the world and Markko wines were always on his list.

Leon D. Adams
(February 1, 1905 – September 14, 1995)

Picture 24: Arnie Esterer (left) and Leon Adams (right)

The story of Markko Vineyards would not be complete without a discussion of the importance of Leon D. Adams (see Picture 24 above) and his influence on Markko. He may have single handedly put Markko on the national stage of great wineries in his book *The Wines of America* first published in 1973.

Leon David Adams was an American journalist, publicist, historian, founder of The Wine Institute and the Society of Medical Friends of Wine.[23] Leon authored numerous books on the history of wine in America, including *The Wines of America*, *The Commonsense Book of Wine* and *The Commonsense Book of Drinking*. As Howard G. Goldberg said in the obituary he wrote about Leon Adams for the *New York Times* back on September 16, 1995, "Leon D. Adams, considered by wine aficionados and the wine industry to be the seminal wine historian in the United States in the 20th century…For Mr. Adams, wine was more than a beverage, it was a cause. In his writing and speeches -- friend and foe alike often found him inspiring and usually crusty -- he said that wine was a civilizing force."[22] Leon was the 1973 recipient of the American Wine Society Award of Merit.

On numerous visits, Arnie would talk about his old friend, Leon Adams. During one visit in December of 2016, we sat in Arnie's office and he pulled out Leon's book *The Wine of America*. Arnie said, "Lucie Morton, who was the AWS Award of Merit recipient in 1994 and a famous viticulturist, brought Leon Adams out here to Markko. Leon was one of Markko's first big promoters. Leon wrote a number of books, one of which was on the medical benefits of wine. Leon was here in November1973 and wrote an inscription in his *The Wines of America* book he gave me." The inscription reads "For Arnulf Esterer, who made the finest '72 White Riesling in America." Remember, Markko's first vintage of Riesling was 1972. Arnie couldn't receive any higher praise than that. In Leon's book "*The Wines of America*", second edition, page 98, in talking about Arnie and Markko Vineyard, Leon says:

> "The little Markko Vineyard and winery were four years old when I happened by in October of 1973 and sampled its 1972 Riesling from the cask. I was amazed; its fresh Riesling fragrance was closer to a young Moselle than any dry American Riesling I have tested yet. My notes made that afternoon read: "Is it an accident? Can he duplicate this wine? Esterer's later vintages of Riesling have approached the 1972 in quality."[1]

Arnie continued "Leon had a sense about what would be helpful to the industry. He was great at promoting our industry and wanted to carry the ball. Leon was a marketing guy and he knew how the wine industry in California got started. He wanted to promote and do public relations (PR) for this area in the east. He was a national figure in the development of wine in this country. He had great things to say about what was going on in the eastern wine region after he visited with Dr. Frank. I remember in Detroit at the AWS meeting, Leon talking about Markko's 1972 Riesling and he said "This is the greatest Riesling in North America." He was the motivator for Markko making super Rieslings."

Leon Adams was a staunch proponent for the American wine industry throughout the 1970's until his death in 1995. He was one of the first to document the history of American wines and he was a great supporter of Arnie and Markko Vineyard. The United States was becoming a wine country and wine sales were out actually out-selling beer in Leon's time. During the session that celebrated Dr. Frank at the 2017 American Wine Society conference, Arnie reminded everyone of one Leon's famous quotes "Wine should be cheaper than milk."

Joseph (Joe) Cooper (1929 – June 4, 2010)

Picture 25: Joe Cooper on the left; Arnie on the right

DOUG MOORHEAD, BILL KONNERTH, BROTHER DAVID
PETRY, ALLEN HOLMES, LEON ADAMS AND JOE COOPER

Back in May of 2016, Arnie told me the story of how a letter from
Joe Cooper (see Picture 25), former Past President of the International
Wine & Food Society – Columbus Branch convinced him the wine
business was for him. Arnie said, "Did I tell you about Joseph and
Jane Cooper of Pincherry Pottery in Columbus, Ohio? Joe Cooper was
the President of The International Wine & Food Society at that time
and was a judge at the Ohio State Fair for wines in 1971. We won 1st
prize for our 1969 Chardonnay that we exhibited there and I received
a letter from Joe Cooper congratulating me. I had been thinking about
whether I wanted to stay in the wine business and his letter was in-
strumental in convincing me to do it, move forward."

I never had to chance to meet Joe but after reading his on-line obituary, I can see why Arnie considered Joe a dear friend. Here's a portion
of Joe's obituary:

> "A man of many aspects, Joe pursued his vocations and avo-
> cations with singular intensity and passion - not being one for
> half measures. Air Force Captain, graduate scholar of English
> literature and linguistics at OSU, Battelle researcher, Professor
> of Sociology at Dennison University, lover of fine food, wine
> and chamber music, baker, organic vegetable and herb gar-
> dener, potter, apiarist and avid reader; there was hardly a sub-
> ject that escaped his ken."[23]

Joe and Arnie started a friendship that day in September 1971 which
lasted until Joe's passing June 4, 2010 at the age of 81.

CHAPTER 5

What matters is what's in the bottle – Arnie's impact on Ohio and beyond

ONE OF MY favorite lines Arnie dropped on me over the last four years of this "labor of love" was a comment that Dr. Frank told Arnie in one of those first meetings back in the late 1960's, "Do as I do and you will succeed. If you succeed, give me the credit. If you fail, it's your fault." As Dr. Frank told Arnie on his first visit to Hammondsport "You have to get rid of hybrids. If you have second rate grapes, you get second rate wines." Dr. Frank vigorously fought to prove that only vinifera varietal grapes make the best wine in the world, period. In Dr. Frank's letter to Arnie dated December 15, 1970, he reinforced the importance of vinifera wines and the success he and his cooperators had growing the vinifera varietals and making them into the best wines. Dr. Frank said:

> "Our goal is to present proofs that the people of this prosperous and magnificent country, America, do deserve to have and to enjoy the best wine world..."

> "...During our twenty years of enjoyment of our life here in

America, we have presented the proofs that these, the best grape varieties, responsible for the highest, premium quality wines, like the famous German Johannisberg Riesling, Gewürztraminer and the most famous Pinot Gris, Pinot Chardonnay, Pinot Noir, which are responsible for the top quality French Burgundies, and the king of the French Bordeaux wines, Cabernet Sauvignon, as well as the four best Russian grape varieties, were never grown so vigorously, productively, and flourishingly, producing the highest quality wines in their native countries, as they do grow in Hammondsport, New York, and in nine other eastern states by more than fifty of my cooperators."[24]

Arnie has been an avid proponent of making quality wine from vinifera grapes because they produce the best all-around wine. As a cooperator of Dr. Frank, it couldn't be any other way. During a visit in August 2015, Arnie said "Dr. Frank said the future of the wine industry was based on the quality of the grapes. Vinifera was the best quality." Arnie continued "if you do the job right and make quality wines, you will make it. You can't be everything to everyone. Find your niche." My interpretation of what Dr. Frank was conveying to Arnie and his cooperators was that European vinifera varietal grapes make the best quality wine.

Arnie's Impact on the Ohio Wine Industry - Quality

In January 2016, I met with a very old and dear friend of Arnie's, Mario Guarraccino. Mario has known Arnie for more than 40 years. During our talk, Mario discussed Arnie's passion for making the best wine he can. Mario said "Most of the wineries around here are making the money with the food, not the wine. Arnie's wines are vintages, while most wines around here taste the same year after year. Arnie's wines are out of the range of the common ones around here. Arnie's Chardonnay, Riesling, Cabernet and Pinot Noir are the best in this region and can compete with any in this country. Arnie makes wine that Dr. Frank would be proud of; he does it slowly and follows the old French ways. He could make more money but it's not about money with Arnie. It's about what goes into the bottle. The quality of the wine represents what this area can do. Arnie is considered the father of Ohio vinifera wines by many other Ohio winemakers and I would certainly agree with that statement."

Greg Johns bolstered Mario's position about why the quality of the wine is more important to Arnie than making money when he said to me, "The problem with the people promoting Ohio wines is that it's about how many bottles can we sell, that's their bottomline. Arnie has not been about how many bottles he can sell. Half the crop rots or is dropped in the vineyard. It's about the quality of the wine...what's in the bottle. Arnie has dumped more wine over the bank than you would believe because it is not worth selling. He has enough balls to dump it over the bank. Other winemakers would just blend it and call it a day...let the cash register ring. He could probably sell it to another winery but he doesn't. If he did sell it the label on the back would have a Markko reference and that won't fly with Arnie. Arnie says the Markko label and what's in the bottle is what counts."

The more I spoke with Greg on that warm August 2018 day, the more he had to say. Greg continued, "I want to expand on one thing I said before about Arnie. He has never been about making money. That has not been his focus. Arnie's focus has been the vineyard and the wines. You can talk to him all you want about making money, but aside from wanting to have the highest price point in the region, that's not his focus. He might have the highest price point but he's not making 40,000 gallons of wine; his focus is on quality."

Greg stops and wants to add another point about Arnie and his character. "He has also had a lot of focus on his workers here. So many of his workers are what I would call unemployable. They are difficult people to employ, people with problems...whether it be alcoholism or drug abuse, broken families or being abused themselves. We all have stories but some of his workers have really tough stories. If they are going through a tough time, you might not see them for a month, 2 months, 6 months and they'll come back and Arnie will welcome them with open arms and give them a job. I think Arnie was really hoping that one of them would be a shining star to take over Markko, like Linda's son, Denis. I think Arnie would have done anything for him, sent him to college, taught him everything but Denis fell into drugs and had a tragic death. Arnie sees something in people that most people don't and gives them a chance, in some cases multiple, multiple, multiple chances. Arnie gets burned so many times by them that it's not funny, but he doesn't give up on them. He thinks everyone has a purpose. This is a cost of doing business that Markko has accepted. It is a problem if you are trying to be efficient."

I asked Greg if Markko would cease to exist, what the impact on the wine industry in the Northeast corner of Ohio would be. Greg said, "Markko is really a cornerstone of quality wine in Ohio. Not only does everybody know Arnie, they know Markko wines. If someone was heading to France to visit family and they wanted to take a bottle of wine, you would send them here to Markko to find one. The thing is anyone who takes over Markko Vineyard is going to want to change some things. Depending on the person or the people, the change could be minimal or it could be drastic to the point where you wouldn't even recognize this place. They could put a slushy machine in the back if they felt like it. It would do a disservice to the legacy of Markko. If whoever takes over Markko gets into the same winemaking stylistic approach as most of the other wineries, their wines could be like anybody else's and if the wines are like everyone else's, why would you drive the extra 30 miles? That's the honest truth of the matter. To buy Markko Vineyard, it can't be about money. You've got to be young, willing to listen to Arnie, and ask questions. It will take time. You need two or three years of being coached, being quiet and listening."

Arnie's influence on Ohio winemaking is out there, you just have to look for it. Arnie was a first generation cooperator of Dr. Frank and the only one in Ohio. We lost Dr. Frank back in 1985 so he wasn't around for the second and third generation cooperators in Ohio. Arnie was there and mentored the next generation, such as Wes Gerlosky at Harpersfield, Art & Doreen Pietrzyk at St. Joseph Vineyard, and Larry Laurello at Laurello Vineyards. You even have the third generation with Matt & Tara Meineke at M Cellars. As Greg Johns told me a number of different times "It's through Arnie we have the second and third generation because they would have never met Dr. Frank." Arnie always gives Dr. Frank the credit, even for the winemakers he has mentored.

During Arnie's 50 plus years, many winemakers, students, wine writers and wine experts have come through the doors of Markko. If I were to write about all of them, this book would end up as an Encyclopedia with multiple volumes. Let's focus on a few key people who have left a positive mark on Markko and the wine industry.

Hélène Mingot (Technical Director, Winemaking / Winegrowing for Eisele Vineyard which is owned by Chateau Latour)

Picture 26: Hélène Mingot

Arnie has had a number of students come through and intern at Markko over the years and none more important in Arnie's opinon than Hélène Mingot (see Picture 26 above) from France. During my first visit with Arnie in August 2015, he wanted to tell me the story of Hélène Mingot. After pouring the proverbial glass of Markko wine, Arnie began to speak. "I have a great story on Hélène. In 1998, Hélène, who was 21 at the time, came from France. She was in the Engineering/Agriculture school there and wanted to be in perfume. She failed the test for that but passed to be in the wine school. I got an email from her when she was in her senior year; she asked if I need 4 months of help and I said sure. Fast forward, she shows up

77

and she said who do you live with? I said by myself. I gave her a room down the hall with her own bathroom and then we went to work together every day. I went to Canada for 2 – 3 weeks and that's when Linda worked with her. After spending time with Hélène, Linda's palate became more refined. Hélène had a super palate and her impact on Linda and Markko was felt from that day forward. Hélène went back to France, graduated, went to Italy and married a guy in Chianti, who had a sailboat/yacht and vineyards. Later, she moved to California and became the winemaker for Derenoncourt California in Napa valley. She was working for one of the most famous winemakers from France named Stéphane Derenoncourt and she made all his wines. She was in charge of both the vineyard and winery. She did everything and worked there for about six years until her green card was up, and she would have to return to France. Before leaving the US, Hélène flew here to Markko and helped us taste some wine. I got her an interview with Randy Ullom of Kendall-Jackson, but Hélène didn't get hired. Years later, after Linda had died, I needed someone to taste the Cabernet barrels. So, I got back in touch with Hélène Mingot; she was back in the US working in California for the Artemis group at Araujo Vineyards (Eisele Vineyard) which is owned by Chateau Latour. She's now in charge of their vineyard and winery in the US and is the Technical Director of Winegrowing and Winemaking. I said, I need a favor, can you come and taste some wines for me and she did."

The winery Hélène Mingot works for today is a 40 acre vineyard in California. They make approximately 8000 cases of wine per year. According to Arnie "It is bio-dynamic and she makes the compost." Hélène told Arnie that Latour paid approximately $110M for 40 acres, which is a bit more than Arnie's and Tim's $14,000 per acre for Markko's 130 acres.

The impact Hélène Mingot had on Markko, especially Linda, was evident. Under Hélène's tutelage, Linda learned to hone her testing abilities and to realize how important the palate is. The tasting is in the nose not just the palate. As Arnie said "The nose is most important." Thanks to Hélène, Markko has produced some of the best Cabernet Sauvignon year after year outside of California.

Randy Ullom (Winemaster for Kendall-Jackson Winery)

Another famous winemaker with connections to Markko Vineyard is Randy Ullom. Randy Ullom is currently the Winemaster for Kendall-Jackson Winery, one of the biggest wineries in the world. The Winemaster is the head winemaker of all the winemakers of Kendall-Jackson. Randy was promoted to that position in 1997.[25]

Arnie stated "Randy spent time at Markko learning about winemaking and went on to be a graduate of Ohio State. Randy wanted to be my winemaker; however, that job was filled already by me. Randy went to work at Johnson Estates for three years and then came to me saying he's going to California to be a winemaker. In 1993, Randy was indeed a winemaker in California for Kendall-Jackson. He came back a couple of years later to visit me and brought a few bottles of wine for me to taste. Years later Jess Jackson of Kendall-Jackson (KJ) appeared on the cover of an edition of the *Wine Spectator*. Within the article on the KJ vineyard, there was Randy running a 1,500 acre vineyard and he was the winemaker. The guy was amazing. He would come in for lectures and he was honored at a banquet recognizing him as a great Ohio State graduate. At this event, I was sitting next to Bobby Moser, who was the VP for Agricultural Administration & Dean at Ohio State University at the time. Looking at Randy's resume, he is Winemaster for Kendall-Jackson, which is the second or third largest winery in the world. He has 40 winemakers and 25 wineries in the world all under him, including some in Chile and Australia. Randy and I are still good friends to this day."

Dr. Roland Riesen (Professor of enology since 2010, Changins – School of viticulture and Enology)

Picture 27: Dr. Roland Riesen – Picture courtesy of HES-SO Master, Changins – School of viticulture and Enology website https://www.hes-so.ch/en/viticulture-enology-398.html

Dr. Roland Riesen (see Picture 27 above) currently is a Professor of Viticulture & Enology at Ecole dingeniers de Changins in Switzerland, and has been since 2010. Dr. Riesen's areas of expertise are in analytical chemistry and grape must and wine aroma chemistry and analysis.[26] According to Arnie and Greg Johns, Dr. Riesen was a major contributor to the Ohio wine industry. They felt he was under appreciated during his time working at the Ohio State University (OSU) Ohio Agricultural Research and Development Center (OARDC) in Wooster, Ohio. Dr. Riesen spent time with Arnie between 1991 until around 2009 while working at ORACD and later when he was with Youngstown State University. From the discussions I've had with Arnie, it is clear they both learned much from each other and really enjoyed talking wine shop whenever they could.

During my first interview with Arnie back in August 2015, Arnie was telling me how he first met Dr. Riesen in the Finger Lakes many years ago. Arnie said "I remember a visit to McGregor Vineyards in the Finger Lakes one time and there was this kid working in the cellar. I asked who he was and he said I'm Roland Riesen. Then I asked him where he was from and he replied Switzerland. He was working at McGregor as an intern. Ohio State hired a wine maker and they hired him. Roland had a Ph.D. and was a great winemaker who worked for Dr. James F. Gallander, Ohio State's California winemaker. Gallander was actually an Enologist and so was Roland. Roland was a great taster with a wonderful palate, but he did not have great communication skills. He was a quiet sort of guy who made beautiful Pinot Gris. Roland was not one of the "good old boys" at OSU, so they let him go. He then went to Youngstown State. After a stint there, he went back to Switzerland where he taught French and then moved on to Ecole dingeniers de Changins in Luzon, Switzerland, where he is today. Roland proved you could grow and make a beautiful Pinot Gris right here in Ohio. Remember, Dr. Frank said the greatest of the vinifera grapes was Pinot Gris. The idiots at OSU couldn't get it. Roland fought the same battle as Dr. Frank, only 30 some years later. Will they ever learn?"

Arnie continued, "This past July 19, 2018, the tri-county grape growers brought Roland back to speak to them about Pinot Gris. We wanted a name from outside this country, an expert. Roland has finally gained the recognition he deserves that was way overdue."

Arnie's Impact on the Ohio Wine Industry – What should he be remembered for?

When doing research for this book, I asked everyone what they would want Arnie to be remembered for. The answer had no boundaries. It could be about wine, his character, his humanity to others or whatever they thought it should be. I couldn't document all the responses;

however, I selected these which I believe capture the essence of who Arnie Esterer truly is.

Greg Johns: During my last interview with Greg Johns (see Picture 28 below) who has known Arnie since 1985, I posed the question about what he felt Arnie should be remembered for. Greg's answers are never short winded but always special. Greg said, "One of the key things is Arnie is a stubborn German and we have butted heads over different things about winemaking or personal things or whatever, but his stubbornness has helped him stay true to his course. He could have easily started making a bunch of sweet wine because half the people who come into a winery in Ohio want a sweet wine. Arnie believes if the wine tells him it's going to be sweet then he may produce a sweet wine periodically. Whether it is a Riesling or a Late Harvest Select Chardonnay, he is not going to dump sugar back into it just to appease them. Arnie has always said the grapes tell you what they want you to do in the vineyard and the wines tell you what they want to be in the cellar. Don't fight it."

Picture 28: Greg Johns (left) with son Alex

Greg continued, "In 2003 Arnie made Sparkling wine with the Riesling. That year's temperatures were crazy cool and when the Riesling came in as a still wine, it would take the enamel off your teeth. It was very acidic. I would have loved to have seen him make all of it into sparkling wine because that was a great year for sparkling Riesling but he did reserve some back and made a still wine out of it. The 1997 vintage was that way too and even when it was bottled it was unpalatable. If you open the still wine now, either the 1997 or 2003 it's really come around and turned into a nice wine. They will stay nice in the bottle for another 20 years. I had some of the 1997 Riesling about a month ago here and it was fantastic."

Greg finished up by noting the difference between Arnie and the rest of the winemakers in the region. "There are others in these regions that are making some nice wines. They looked to Arnie for advice and suggestions but many of our wineries are fiscally impatient. When Arnie talks to them about leaving the wine Sur lie in the barrel for two years, they will instantly say they can't afford to do it." Sur lie is the French expression for "on the lees" where the lees is the coarse sediment, which consists mainly of dead yeast cells and small grape particles that accumulate during fermentation.[27] Greg continued, "They may have a half dozen reasons why they need to get it in the bottle quickly whereas Arnie leaves it in the cask for two years on the Sur lie. Because of this he gets body, roundness and maturity in his wines that others don't. Even though they are making good wines, they are not hitting the level that the Markko wines have hit. Assuming you have cellar space, if you leave the wine in the barrel or cask for an extra year or two, you can add 50¢ or $1 a bottle and still could be at your same price point. If they achieve the increase in quality that Arnie's been able to, it would allow them to charge a much higher price. The system does pay for itself but you can't convince them."

Arnie Esterer: I couldn't finish this section without having posed the same question to Arnie...what would you like people to remember about Arnie Esterer? Arnie said, "You know that we, Markko, led the way. We are doing research and trying to show where the potential is and how we can make better wine in this region. It's following Dr. Frank and following some of his thinking and passing it on to the next generation. We're just trying, you know, to be grape growers and wine-growers. That's a Philip Wagner word "winegrower". It's growing the grape to make wine with the end product being more important than the steps in the middle. Like my father and mother, we are research-ers. This is a 50 plus year research endeavor. My dad got a Ph.D. and I wanted a Ph.D. but they don't give Ph.D.'s much in agriculture. I think getting that degree would have made my father happy though. I just carry on as though I'm doing a thesis. This is a work in progress. There are questions to ask, some are answered and some are not. We con-tinue questioning in order to make better wines. It is not a competition. I'm not up against Chalet Debonne or St. Joseph's vineyards. I don't want to beat them, I'm just trying to make Chardonnay the way we make it and continue to make it better. The grapes are grown here, fermented here into wine, bottled and sold here. It's a whole story in itself. You could bring me a California wine and ask if mine is as good as it is, but you either like it better or you don't. Each has their person-alities. There's room for everybody and some people are afraid of that. If this region and city of Conneaut became an area known for its wine, we could have 10, 20 different growers as we almost have 1,000 acres of good vineyard land between Under Ridge and South Ridge right through the city. It's all elevated and you can see the lake. There are some beautiful sites in there. We've got 500 acres right around us. It would take a generation or two to build."

Arnie's Odds and Ends

In spending time with Arnie and recording 99% of our conversations, there's a ton of good stuff in those recordings. The problem is if I wrote about all of it, I might never finish this book. To address this dilemma, here are a few "odds and ends" of interesting topics and discussions I have had with Arnie. They range from discussions about the vineyard, to the three tier system, to Markko's Riesling and a few others but all are worthy of sharing.

Arnie Documents…Everything!

If you have ever taken a peek into Arnie's office, you would see he keeps everything. You might say he is a pack rat. The truth is he does keep everything and that includes documenting the history of every vine in the vineyard. Arnie rates every vine or plant on a spreadsheet and has been doing this since the beginning of Markko Vineyard. The rating system judges each vine on a scale between 0 and 6 with 6 being the highest rating. Zero means the vine is dead and 1 is a root stock. There were two "selections by nature" as Arnie called it for the vines in 2014 and 2015. Arnie said "If they survived the polar vortex then they are hardy plants and some did." Arnie's documentation fetish is the researcher/scientist in him. Arnie told me hundreds of time the most important job is to grow the grapes, get some indication of what the vine can do and then start concentrating on the grapes to do their best. One time in 2016 while we were walking out to the vineyard, Arnie said, "This region needs to find the best wine, the best varietal. You don't need to push every kind of grape there is. The French were thinking all the time to find your best grape and do one thing and do it well. If it's a good wine you can find a use for it. I once visited the Christian Brothers in Napa valley. They had 23 wines, so I asked which one is best. Their answer was they're all good. That's just bullshit! Our region, NE Ohio, needs to find the grapes that are going to do the best to make the best possible wine we can. That's why I write everything down. You think I can remember what was going on in 1974?" Arnie has such a way with words!

Arnie talking about the vineyard: Location matters

In November 2015, Arnie and I walked out and toured the vineyard. Arnie said "I own 250 acres in Conneaut of which only 10 – 12 acres are under grapes. We deep plowed a number of rows three feet down and put top soil on the bottom. By doing this, you get no weeds for the first four years. You mound around the base of the vines in the winter to protect the roots. Snow is a good thing as it acts like insulation. We have variations from plant to plant and don't know if it's the soil from spot to spot, location in the vineyard, different root stock, or a warmer part in the vineyard...don't totally know. We take cuttings from the vines that survived and propagate them. It takes four to five years before we get any grapes from them. We make grafts and put them in the green house for a year before planting them in the vineyard. We have done a number of trials, trench vs. deep plow and tried different root stocks with Chardonnay recently in Row 16. In Row 5, we have Dr. Frank's Muscat, a Russian white table grape. We planted some of it with Chardonnay in between. It ripens really early and has great flavor. I think understanding what the vineyard is doing, and what the potential is, is very important. The first vineyard was planted in 1969 in the mid-high section. We re-planted in 1971, with rows running east to west. You can see Lake Erie from here in the vineyard. We are 3.5 miles south of the lake and 225 feet above the lake. That relationship is important to our success. The woods also have an impact on the vines. We need to make sure the vines get plenty of sunshine, especially in the morning, so we cleared out some of the big trees. We tried spacing the rows ten feet apart and that was a mistake. Nine foot rows are the way to go. We create our own compost and it's organic. One big question we have is why did a particular vine survive the 2014 and 2015 hard winters, the Polar Vortex years? Is it the stock, the soil, or the location in the vineyard? It appears to be resistant to cold so we want that one. We don't totally know but will make cuttings from it. Wine grapes fruit out in three years and the fourth year you can get a whole crop. Row 3 is where Tim Hubbard's ashes were spread. We have Pinot Noir planted there, and it is now known as the Tim Hubbard Vineyard. Pinot does well in Row 3...thanks Tim."

Arnie talking about Markko Riesling

During our conversation in January 2016, Arnie wanted to talk about what makes his Riesling Markko Riesling. Arnie said "Question, how do you make a Riesling with the right qualities? What makes it a Markko Riesling? It's the Sur lie or the dead yeast. Markko's 2009 Riesling sat in the tank on the Sur lie for over 6 years undisturbed and we just bottled it in October 2015. It was the longest on the Sur lie for a Riesling Markko has done. Our 2007 and 2008 Rieslings were super but a bit sweet. What makes a wine dry? Well, less sugar. You have to let it finish longer in the stainless tank. Some German guys do it in barrels. The longer you leave it in the tank, the more the sugar ferments out. Oh, one more thing. Ohio can ripen a Riesling better than Finger Lake wineries in New York. We have 184 days of growing season in NE Ohio but there are only160 days in the Finger Lakes region. Riesling is a great grape because you can make it sweet or dry and everything in between."

Dr. Frank's Visit – Some advice for Arnie

I once asked Arnie if Dr. Frank had ever visited Markko. Arnie said "Oh, he came by here one time. We had Riesling in a Burgundy bottle and he didn't like that. Dr. Frank said if looks like a dog, acts like a dog and talks like a dog, it's a dog, but this doesn't look like a Riesling because it is in the wrong bottle". Markko changed bottles the next year."

Arnie's thoughts on what makes a wine last long in the bottle

I asked Arnie about what makes a wine last a long time in a bottle. He said, "It's in the preservatives and how the wine is made…the acidity, alcohol and tannins. All of these are preservatives. The secret is you have to have good acidity in wine. The grapes have to be ripe but not over ripe. If they are over ripe, they age in the bottle too soon and won't last. At Dr. Frank's and at Markko, we barely get the grapes ripe when we bring them in. If you leave the wine on the Sur lie longer, you get much more aging and the wine is able to withstand oxygenation. You get the cytoplasm in the wine, age on the oak, grape seed, stem, skins and oak tannins; they are all phenols or preservatives. They help keep the oxygen off the wine because oxygen is a killer of good wine and needs to be kept away as much as possible throughout the wine making process. California has many more growing days which is good for Cabs and that helps in the aging process. Bottle aging helps the tannins calm down so the more tannins you have the longer the wine will last in the bottle. The year has an impact on the longevity of the wine as well."

Arnie went on to say, "The longer you can age the wine in the barrel, the more you can charge. There are differences from new and old oak. By toasting wood, you change the character, and the oak provides the tannins which kill a lot of the bad stuff and adds preservatives (phenols) to help the aging of the wine. When you make Cab, how long should you keep it in the barrel? Two years? Linda said three is better. We've been using 1/3 new oak. We leave red wine, in a barrel for one year...then we rack it the second year. Racking is moving the wine to another barrel but leaving the crud behind. As an example, for Cabernet in 2016, we used 12 barrels, 4 new and 8 old ones. We want to go with all new oak in the future...fresh and clean to get all the tannins."

The once famous Maisonette Restaurant served Markko Wines

The former Maisonette Restaurant, which first opened in 1949, was one of North America's most highly rated restaurants. It was last owned by the Comisar family before it closed its doors on July 25, 2005.[28] The Maisonette had, at one time, the longest running streak of five-star awards and only ended at 41 years due to its closure.[28] In June of 2016, Arnie talked proudly about having his wine on the wine list at this five-star restaurant. Arnie said, "The Maisonette Restaurant in Cincinnati was the famous 5-star restaurant that sold Dr. Frank and Markko wines. Yes, Markko wines. It started when I used to sell wine to a radiologist in Cincinnati, who had a mansion off Edwards Avenue that looked out over the Ohio River. He would buy a couple of cases and I would drive them down to him. At Maisonette, we started in the Normandy room downstairs, not the top spot of the restaurant. I was doing a tasting on a river boat in Kentucky and this guy, one of the Comisar family members from Maisonette, invited us to the restaurant. I walked in and said I was a cooperator of Dr. Frank and he tasted our wines. After that we were in. I would sell over in Kentucky at the Cork and Bottle and Party Source and would sell to David Schelkneckt, who was one of Robert Parker's right hand men at the time. David was the buyer for the Party Source and he bought a lot of Markko wine. David had a super palate."

Arnie – the most fun about being a winemaker

One of the first questions I ever asked Arnie was what he considered the most fun about being a winemaker. I thought it was a good question and it turns out I was right. Arnie said "Excellent question! For me it's the research and watching the vines grow and how they adapt to the area here. I talk to the vines all the time. But foremost, it is figuring out how we can make them grow well here. If we grow them well, then we make the wine. I feel like a researcher just like my mother and father. My mother did research in biochemistry and my father did research in pulp and paper chemistry. I love the research side and of course I love wine".

Arnie's thoughts on the recent growth of wineries in Ohio

Arnie wanted to discuss the growth of hybrids and the *Ohio Farm Winery Liquor Permit*, passed in 2016. According to an article by Peggy Kirk Hall, Associate Professor of Agricultural and Research Law, on the Ohio State University's Farm Office website "The new Ohio Farm Winery Permit legally designates the wine as being made from grapes grown on the wine maker's farm. Sponsors and supporters of the legislation claim that the special designation will help consumers know a wine's localized nature, bring recognition to Ohio's wine growing regions, keep Ohio competitive with other states that designate farm-produced wines, and ensure that farm wineries continue to receive property tax treatment as agricultural operations."[29] Arnie said "That's huge. The bad thing is they are doing hybrids. They have come up with a new law in Ohio, a new license called *Ohio Farm Winery Liquor Permit*, so I need to get mine transferred over and become a farm winery. They are going to give us benefits as a farm winery that the others won't get. They are going to segregate licenses for those growing the grapes and making wine here in Ohio from those who acquire their grapes/juice from sources outside of the state. Growing grapes is very labor intensive. If this whole region grows hybrids, we will get a reputation and will never really be able to compete with other wines in the world. Again, Dr. Frank was against hybrids. We have vinifera here but some of the wineries are doing hybrids. If you get into Lake Erie and are doing something else other than vinifera, you are not helping us."

Arnie's thoughts on types of vinifera grapes to grow in the Lake Erie region

In October of 2017, Arnie and I discussed his thoughts on the type of vinifera grapes that would grow and make excellent wine in the NE region of Lake Erie. Arnie has over 50 years of experimenting and data to support and back his opinion. Arnie said "Riesling will not be our best grape because the climate always changes around October 1st. Chardonnay always seems to come in, in great shape, even if we get rain throughout the season. It doesn't seem to affect Chardonnay. We are going to keep Pinot Gris in our blend of Chardonnay. We are going to use the term "Homage" more and more. I believe that is our signature. Chardonnay is in the Pinot family and everyone is talking Pinot and trying to make Pinot Noir. Though growers around here want to make this a Pinot region, we make dynamite Cabernet Sauvignon here and have been for a long time. Instead of going to Cabernet Sauvignon, we might want to go to Merlot. Merlot for our type of trellis grows higher and ripens earlier than Cab. Merlot ripens earlier but is winter sensitive. It buds out earlier than Cab so it gets killed easier. The question then is whether the extra risk is worth taking."

Arnie finished up by discussing the grapes grown and wine made at Markko. Arnie said "We are doing Conneaut Creek style wines. This is USA Conneaut Ohio wine. Wine is a location. We need a signature grape, Chardonnay or, for some around here, Pinot Gris. It should be some grape from the Pinot family as they ripen the same time as Concord which I judge against. All Markko Chardonnay has some Pinot Gris in it but not sure how much. Linda didn't like Pinot Gris by itself."

Arnie's thoughts on the Three Tier system

During one of my last interview visits (October 2018) with Arnie, I wanted his thoughts on the "Three Tier System" as it has been called. The Three Tier System is how wine is sold in America after prohibition. The three tiers are 1) Producers – growers of grapes and wineries that make the wine, 2) Wholesalers – importers and distributors who acquire the wine from the producers and 3) Retailers – restaurants and retailers who acquire the wines from the wholesalers and sell to you and me. I figured after 50 some years of dealing with the system, Arnie would have some insightful thoughts, so I asked him about it. Arnie said, "Very important. It is a way to distribute wine. Actually, that is one of the best questions you have asked because there is no one answer to say the three tier system is right or wrong. The system works when you are moving a lot of wine out of California. You can move it, you can bring the juice here, the grapes here; they've done everything. When you're selling, I think it is the difference between, small, medium and big wineries. The little winery can't get into the three tier system, there's no room for it. We have 50 states and every state basically has their own laws. What I think is really stupid about the three tier system is the large distributors, like Southern Wines, who distribute wines in 40 states, object to Direct to Consumer (DTC) sales because they think we're going to steal their business. I only have one case of wine to sell, while they have hundreds or thousands of cases coming out of California going to the people who want it, so why should the big guys restrict the little guys? There is room for both of us. If I want to ship a bottle of Markko to a customer in whatever state, I should be able to but that is not necessarily the case today. The three tier system is good for the big distributor. Gallo can move trains loads of wine out and hand it out but the little guy can't. For example, I can't sell my wine in New York State. I have to have a license to sell wine there and it would cost me $300. How many cases of wine am I going to sell in New York? Not many, so I can't start out with $300 in the hole. If I don't have a license, UPS is going to dump the wine. The three tier system benefits the big guys and distributers who determine what wines can go where. The distributers have their position in that they can be most efficient when they are moving pallets and truck loads of wine. But for one or two cases, they don't care. The problem with licenses is every state is so different and costs are too high. We have been fighting state by state for years. One time I sent a case of wine to a customer in North Carolina and the Attorney General sent me a letter saying I can't solicit the shipment of wines in North Carolina. UPS or FedEx won't pick up wine that is going to New York from here because they know I don't have a license. I was asked by the American Wine Society to submit some wines for the November 2018 meeting in Buffalo but how could I do it? Would I have to drive them up to Buffalo myself? What a system. Again the system is good for the distributors and big wineries but basically hoses the little guy."

Arnie talked about his tribute to Dr. Konstantin Frank

In October 2018, Arnie talked about one of his tributes to Dr. Frank. Arnie said "Homage Chardonnay at Markko was made in honor of Dr. Frank and the first time we made it was in 2010. We donated a dollar a bottle from the sales to the American Wine Society's Educational Foundation." He showed me a bottle saying "This is the next generation, the 2013 vintage. I called it homage because it has some Pinot Gris in it which Dr. Frank said was the greatest wine grape. This Chardonnay was the first one done in all new oak barrels at Markko. This was placed in new barrels Sur lie for three years and never racked. The juice was pressed in whole bunches and sat for 24 hours and then was pumped into a brand new barrel. They were Grand Cru barrels made by Canton Cooperage. The wine stayed in for three years, was never touched but was topped off periodically. I'm a lazy winemaker. After three years, we bottled it. You have the advantage of Sur Lie, umami, body and other things. We are trying to modify that slightly. Do you want to hear about all my mistakes? Romaine Conte's book tells you exactly how to do Pinot Noir and Chardonnay. I was reading through the part on Pinot Noir, it said to fine it with three egg whites just before you bottle it. I did that for the Chardonnay. It worked out and it took out some of the excess oak. I turned the page and it said you don't use egg whites in the white wine. What do you use? You use milk, fresh raw milk with no cream and no fat. They injected it into the barrel three weeks before they bottled it. They wait nine months after bottling before they release it to deal with bottle shock. The wine speaks for itself."

Picture 29: Homage Chardonnay label – tribute to Dr. Konstantin Frank

Arnie on why he does not filter his wine

Arnie said "We used to filter the wines. We did sterile filtering and the only thing we filtered was the sweet wine. I've gotten more and more lazy or more traditional. When you look at the filter pads, they are brown, they're gummy and you're taking out all kinds of stuff. Depending on if I'm using a 0.45 micron filter for sweet wine or a 200 micron filter, you're always taking out something. The sediment in the bottle, which we used to filter out, helps the wine last longer in the cellar. That's what the umami is; it protects the wine from oxidation. Umami is one of the five basic tastes together with sweetness, sourness, bitterness, and saltiness. The sediment has the ability to absorb and assimilate oxygen. The reason I stopped filtering is because the wines are better and they are themselves without it. Let the wines speak for themselves. For thousands of years they did not have filters, so screw it."

Arnie talked about the Massachusetts Institute of Technology (MIT) connection

During a visit in August of 2018, Greg Johns was there and asked me "Did Arnie tell you about his MIT connection?" Arnie said "Oh my God, he was just here. He just came last week. Professor Linn Hobbs, Ph.D. is Professor Emeritus of Materials Science and Nuclear Engineering. He was a professor of ceramics. He came from Michigan and his job was to encase Uranium and put it in the Yuka Mountains. He was a ceramics guy but he taught the wine appreciation course at MIT for like 30 years and is still teaching it. He likes Riesling. He said Arnie send me Riesling. He would order lots of Riesling and used it for tastings in his class. We would hear from these students from MIT saying we had your Riesling in our class and we want to get some. We would either ship it or they would come through here." Greg said "I've been here a half dozen times when the students would come through and say we're from MIT." Arnie said "Oh Right. Hobbs would come out and pick up a $1,000 worth of wine and go home with it. He would strip me out of Riesling. He has a Markko dog and now he has a second Markko dog named Whoopi. He has just been a good guy."

A few tidbits about Arnie and Markko Vineyard

1. The first Markko vintages were the 1972 Chardonnay and Riesling with Cabernet Sauvignon in 1975. Pinot Noir was 1983 from what Arnie can remember.

2. The first grapes Markko planted were Riesling and Chardonnay in 1968/1969.

3. Arnie on winemaker's ego: "You know me being humble is all a show too. Question is how can I be humble? I have such a big ego. Everyone has an ego it's just how you treat it."

4. The 2012 Riesling vintage was barrel aged for 4 years in used old barrels, which was another Arnie experiment.

5. During one of my visits to watch the wine pressing operation in action, the following was communicated to me. I promised I would not reveal who told me and I will honor that. "The wine pressing operation for the Cab at Markko is like a chaotic dance of grumpy and funny people, that is well planned and choreographed but sure looks like a play that stinks. However, somehow out of this chaos comes a beautiful, full bodied, dark colored, with perfect acidity and well balanced Cabernet in four years."

6. French winemaker Ali Gharsallah-Nuernberg worked for a short time at Markko in 1986. Arnie remembered the first thing Ali said upon arriving at Markko "I will make Champagne out of whatever your problems are."

Prestigious Honors Arnie has received

Arnie has received many honors over the past 50 years and I sort of promised him I would not talk about them. Well I'm breaking that promise just briefly to talk about two honors he received which deserve mentioning. In 1997, Arnie received the highest honor that the American Wine Society bestows annually at its conference, the Award of Merit. Since 1971 the Award of Merit has been given to wine industry luminaries in recognition of substantial and meritorious contributions in viticulture, enology, education or journalism. Finally, in 2005, Arnie was inducted into the Ohio Wine Producers Association Ohio Wine Hall of Fame. The purpose of the Ohio Hall of Fame is to recognize the outstanding contributions of an individual to the Ohio wine industry, to gain recognition for the excellence in the Ohio industry and to encourage future leaders.[30] Arnie truly is a pioneer for the Ohio wine industry and his tremendous contributions and his legacy will live on for future generations of wine growers and winemakers.

CHAPTER 6

Funny Stories

A BOOK ABOUT Markko Vineyard would be incomplete without adding a few of the many funny things that happened on the way to making some of the best vinifera wines in America. Over the last four years of hanging out with Arnie and the Markko team, I sure have learned a tremendous amount about the operations of a winery and the humor that comes with it. There were a few stories I would love to have included but the editing of the "colorful language" would have ruined them. Instead, here are few "PG" tales that I hope will make you chuckle.

Funny Stories

1. Arnie talking about bottling: "My kids and a couple others would run the bottling line and one day at noon the state inspector for wine shows up and wants to see my permit right away. He goes in the door and sees all the kids working the line and asked if they are all my family. And I said yes, six kids between the ages of 12 to 14. He says good, good to see a family working. Then he turns around and high tails it out of here."

2. Arnie said "Another funny story was another time we were

bottling. The kids were taking some sips. I wasn't here at the time and Linda was in charge. The kids went home roaring drunk...whoops."

3. Arnie talking about a wine license: "We had to get licensed. One day we are working on the paperwork for the license and the federal inspector comes here from the US Treasury ATF out of Cleveland. Tons a paper-work, background checks, no connection with the Mafia, etc. I was a little shook up about it and had a type writer with me. Half way down to the cellar, I dropped it and all the papers went flying. The inspector calmed me down and told me how to fill out the paperwork, where to cut the corners, like if you have 50 gallon barrel, you only count it as 48 gallons, so you go to 60 gallon, you call it 55 gallon. You're going to lose some of the wine in the process. So later, the state guy comes in, a guy named Dwight. This is a bonded winery so the state says you can't taste wine off the premises. So Dwight, in his trench coat, walked around the winery. The federal tax paid area is designated by the red line on a map of Markko. The designated area includes the winery and a patio. Dwight then walked around the woods in a big circle and said this is your patio. So you can take your glass of wine and walk out into the woods, take a leak and walk back. No problem... you're within the red line."

4. Arnie said "We are at a wine conference in Columbus and the then Governor, Bob Taft, is there with his wife, Hope Taft, who is supporting Mothers Against Drunk Driving. Fred Dailey, the Secretary of Agricultural and ex-Marine paratrooper, and Taft are tightening up controls on wine. All the vendors are there at this trade show with their wines and the Liquor Control Board is coming to give an

address at dinner. It was a nice elegant dinner and we all have our wine out there and everyone is excited. I'm out in the hall before dinner and here is Dwight, in a trench coat, and I said how are you and he said working. We all get together in the banquet hall and the Director of Agricultural Control says we are here to help you. All you have to do is follow the rules, etc. and everything will be fine. We come out and Dwight from the State confiscated all of the wine and cited Ohio State University for not having the proper permits. They wanted to shut this thing down. They impounded all of the wine, cases and cases while we are having dinner and had just heard this speech from the Director of Agricultural Control. The hotel had to buy the wine rather than us just serving it for free. We were not following some rule, and we got nailed. Dwight did not want to do it, but it was political so he had to."

5. Arnie talks about Walter Taylor of Bully Hill wine fame. "Walter Taylor was in Detroit when we had the AWS conference there in the early 70's, must have been 1974 or 1975. I sat at a table with him for a while, and he finally decides to taste my Chardonnay. He asked "Is this 100% Chardonnay?" I said yes and that was all he said on that. He got up and walked away. Funny guy!"

6. Greg Johns told a story about one of Arnie tasting groups. "Did Arnie tell you about any of his tasting groups? He is still involved with the one. I remember being a green stick and going to some at Swingos restaurant. This guy who was getting his master sommelier for Vintage Wines was there and Matt Swingo was part of that group. There are some really good tasters in this group and it used to be all these men. This gets back to Linda Frisbie who would then gripe about this tasting group and she called it "The He

Man Women Haters Club". We've all known that tasting group as "The He Man Women Haters Club" ever since."

7. Greg Johns: "A funny story is Arnie sun bathes in the nude to get his vitamin D. He was by the house buck naked and the meter reader came by, female, and well yowzer! That was funny. That can happen any day of the week at Markko."

8. Culetta told a story about Linda Frisbie. "Just before she passed away, Arnie, Jennifer and I were in the wine cellar topping off the barrels and tasting and we decided to pull a fast one on her and got into her Muscat. There is a whole barrel of it down there, so Jennifer took some up to her to taste. She got mad and said "get out of my Muscat". We used to drive her crazy when we put the radio on so she took it one day and hid it from us. She was something else. She always said if you run across any black hoses that are moving don't touch it...it was a snake and his name was George."

9. There is a funny quote attributed to André Tchelistcheff that Arnie showed me in an article in *Wine & Vines* magazine during one of my visits "God made Cabernet Sauvignon but the Devil made Pinot Noir".

10. In October 2018, Arnie was talking to me about marketing. Arnie said "You know we need to advertise the virgin barrel. I could say this is all brand new oak, but who the hell cares about that? Let's say these are all virgin barrels. I can put Cabernet select reserve aged three years in a virgin barrel on the label. Do you think that would get public recognition? Hey I don't do enough marketing; we got to come up with a catch. You know I say aged three

years Sur lie in brand new oak, but who cares? If I said aged three years Sur lie in virgin barrels I guarantee the virgin barrel part would catch their attention. Hey they have virgin olive oil and that's legal. It's not a sexist remark." I said to Arnie "You should do that on the website and say 2016 Cab being released after three years in virgin barrels." Arnie said "I'm going to do that. We might get some attention. I've got these wines entered at the American Wine Society and they are asking for updates on the website and so I can advertise those virgin barrels. Linda once brought in a wine called Big Red Pecker. Dr. Thomas Wykoff, who founded the Cedar Hill Wine Company and the restaurant Au Provence in Cleveland Heights, had a wine called his terminal red. The label is the Terminal Tower in Cleveland with King Kong or the big gorilla on it and his pecker is sticking out. He applied for a Federal permit and they turned him down."

CHAPTER 7

The future of vinifera in the Lake Erie Region

IN JUNE 2016, Arnie and I had our first discussion on possible endings for the book. The ideas revolved around where Arnie thinks the growing of vinifera will be 30 years from now, the future of Markko after Arnie, what he would like people to remember about him and Markko or why Markko is still here. We did not come up with an answer that day nor should we have. Arnie needed time to think and ponder it, which would take another year, before we both agreed on the last chapter.

Arnie's Deal

During our talk that June, Arnie wanted to tell me ultimately why he wanted to start Markko Vineyard and the deal he made with a higher authority. Arnie said "My work here is worship. Let me explain. Starting the vineyard was growing a food and I made a deal with God to work it until I die, whether it was successful or not. This was something that needed to be done for the area, the Western Reserve, and Tim Hubbard was a partner in that. We started out with the need for wine in our society. We tried to get a creed adopted and accepted by the American Wine Society. We spoke with Leon Adams about it and he was supportive but it hasn't happened yet. We believe wine is a food, both healthy and nutritious, to be consumed with meals, a beverage of moderation and not to be abused and sometimes used as a sacrament." The vision Arnie had was influenced by Dr. Frank and Philip Wagner. Both Wagner and Dr. Frank were inspirations but this vineyard is his worship.

Markko – The 50 year demonstration

In the four years I met with Arnie, he always talked about Markko being this experiment or research project on how to grow and make vinifera wines on this plot of land in Conneaut, Ohio. During one such meeting in October 2018, I specifically asked Arnie to expand on the half-a-century experiment. Arnie said "I thought it would only be like 25 years. I like to call it a demonstration. We are demonstrating what Dr. Frank was saying, what the vinifera varieties could do, what the soils and the climate could do. There is an old adage in the farm business, get better before you get bigger. Dr. Frank taught us vinifera could grow here but more importantly, we should try to determine which variety. We needed to determine which clones and which root stocks would work. We had 18 different root stocks so I think this was what Dr. Frank was saying, diversity, I love it. What Markko was doing was looking at different root stocks. The differences in them can be very subtle and reflect how it works in the soil and the contribution of soil to the terrior. Dr. Frank said there are three marriages, 1) the root stock with the soil, 2) the root stock and the scion, like root stock and Chardonnay and how do they get along and 3) the climate. Which clone or which grape variety are you going to use on top. How does it do in this climate? These are the three marriages Dr. Frank spoke about. This was a very important lesson. That's huge! You need a wine that you can produce year to year that is also a quality wine. It depends on the water. I think this is an important factor. Our best Chardonnay is grown in the Marie Vineyard where we took off two feet of top soil with a bulldozer to level off the vineyard. After that, we deep tiled it four feet down and deep ploughed it three feet down. The vines that have the greater water hardiness, that have the best sugars, the best everything with the lowest amount of disease are growing in the sub-soil. I think what we are saying is that grapes don't like rich soils and they don't like a lot of water. They like poor soils like in Germany where the best vines are those struggling in the worst soils. You need to be in poorer soils with not much water to stress the vines. The vines have to go find their water and find their minerals. They don't want to be fat and happy. The vines want to be mean and lean. That's what we did in the Marie vineyard by taking off the top soil. In the mid-hill, the steep hill they all did well there. The French have spent 1,000 years doing it and we're trying to do it for 25 or 50 years."

The Gospel according to Arnie

As stated previously, Arnie needed time to think about what the ending of the book should be. In October 2017, Arnie and I agreed the last chapter would be Arnie's thoughts on the future of vinifera in the Lake Erie Appellation and Ohio. I, not Arnie, decided to call this the Gospel according to Arnie, because he is to me the father of vinifera in Ohio.

Verse 1: The Pinot Belt and the signature grape

Arnie states "The Lake Erie region, this is Pinot. This region, in a sense, is Burgundy. It is Pinot Chardonnay, Pinot Noir and Pinot Gris. I love to do Cab, so we do. Linda had it down but it's not that consistent. Well, actually, it is very consistent. It doesn't have the problems in growing and mold and so it is resistant to that entire sort of thing. We have enough heat here to do Cab. I throw out Merlot as a possibility because it ripens very early and because it will grow on a Trellis like Concord does so, we are trying to figure it out. The Pinot Belt goes around the world at a latitude spanning Burgundy in France to NE Ohio, which includes Pinot Noir, Pinot

Gris, Gamay and Chardonnay or Pinot Chardonnay as it used to be called. The amazing fact is that there are two narrow strips of geography which provide good conditions for growing great Pinots. In the northern hemisphere, Burgundy, parts of Italy, Slovenia, part of northern California and Oregon are prominent but so is the south shore of Lake Erie including the tri-county region of Ashtabula, Lake and Geauga counties. The growers and wineries around here believe Pinot Gris might be our signature grape and are going to promote this region as a Pinot Gris region. We've got seven wineries all of sudden realizing they are making Pinot Gris. They want to focus on that because they want to get attention paid to this region for sales. They are saying let's be known for Pinot Gris. I don't even make Pinot Gris, but we grow it. We are a generation away from figuring that out, how to make it and grow it in this climate and soil...another generation at least. A white grape may be the grape for this region...Chardonnay, Pinot Gris...maybe a red...Pinot Noir. I don't think it will be Riesling. It could be Grüner Veltliner...someday there will be a hybrid grape that will make a better wine and be resistant to diseases and will grow in this climate. I hope Dr. Frank doesn't roll over in his grave after me saying that. Pinot Noir, Chardonnay and Pinot Gris could be the signature grapes for this region. My guess is those three may be the ones. Maybe, but only time will tell. It took 50 years to get to that and Dr. Frank was saying long before that Pinot Gris is the greatest of the great vinifera."

Verse 2: The Ohio Wine Region needs a reputation not just tourism

Arnie opined "The region needs to develop a reputation; instead they are going after tourism. They want to bring in great volumes of people, to make some sweet wine and sell it. I do not agree, nor did Dr. Frank, and this is not the answer. You need to make great dry wines so we need to go back to basics. The Ohio region has never had wines in quantity. When Markko started, Ohio was only making one gallon per capita while the national average was two. Other regions in the country, such as California and Washington, were even higher at 4 – 5 gallons per capita. The Ohio Wine Producers Association, particularly, Donnie (Donniella) Winchell did a great job but couldn't see the broad spectrum of marketing levels. What's the most important thing? They need to grow the grapes here. The industry will be based on growing grapes here in Ohio and not just being a winery and trying to attract tourists. If we grow quality vinifera grapes and make excellent wines from them, the tourists will come. There are 70 acres across from Markko that would be excellent for growing grapes. The potential is great here."

Verse 3 – Conneaut is a great wine growing area for vinifera

Arnie truly believes Conneaut, Ohio is a natural area for growing vinifera grapes. Arnie said "It's the location to the lake, the right soil, elevation, the growing season or the terroir. It's loam soil but not really rich soil. It's variable and not too deep but it's not all clay. All of the vineyards, the Concord vineyards that grow here all ripen before the Northeast. In this site and this good soil, with the good exposure to the lake, the topography is right and it's good for grapes. Over in Geneva they are growing grapes all the way down to the lake but when they get too close to water, they don't do very well because it's too wet. When you get over to the North Ridge, which is Route 20 and the South Ridge and you go to those levels where the Glacier had receded, you find sites that are good. The best vineyards down there are about seven miles from the lake and about 1,000 feet above sea level. You can see almost into Cleveland from there. Our site has swales and hollows and we have some problems, but overall it is a really good site. It's as good here at 800 feet as it is on South River Road at 950 or 1,000 feet. I think we have proven that this location can produce some good wine. It's in the grapes but it comes back to Linda and her having a really super palate. We need to get recognition for all the wineries but we need better winemakers. Not that there are not good winemakers here, but they are following the book and not their nose. That's what you find in France, in Burgundy and Bordeaux. I would see farmers siting around in a barn tasting each other's wine. That's what the Tri-County growers are doing here."

Verse 4 – No Mona Lisa in Ohio

In one of our last interviews, Arnie discussed Ohio not having a wine that is leading the pack. He said "Ohio doesn't have a leader, a wine being sold for $100/bottle and getting international press. We don't have anything like that and that's what this area needs. We need someone to get us that recognition. Dr. Frank got recognition in New York and had the PR and publicity although he didn't have the highest priced wine. I believe $35 – $40 is the top price for a bottle of wine from New York. California has the reputation and some wines there are $500 - $1,000 a bottle. Judgment at Paris and beating the French gave them that international recognition. Ohio doesn't have our Mona Lisa yet. The French control the supply and demand and that's how they did it. Romaine-Conte is that example."

Author's Cliff note (see what I did there!?): I would beg to differ with Arnie and so would many of the legions of Markko wine lovers. Arnie's Chardonnay and Cabernet Sauvignon are those Mona Lisa wines. The problem is Markko has not gotten the press or PR needed to promote them as such. Notable wine journals, such as *Wine Enthusiast* and *Wine Spectator* don't give Ohio a second glance. *The Cork Report* wine blog says "*The Cork Report* examines North American wine country with open minds and intrepid palates. We investigate and celebrate the special people and places that make for delicious and distinctive wines... Now, our "beat" has expanded to encompass all of North America, save California, Oregon, and Washington — not because there aren't incredible wines from those places, but because their coverage is ubiquitous."[31]

The Cork Report pretty much covers every other state, including Pennsylvania, but not Ohio.

I'm not saying the *Wine Enthusiast* and *Wine Spectator* don't rate Markko wines, they have. However, the best ratings I've seen in these two wine journals were 88 points for Markko's 2013 Cabernet Sauvignon Select Reserve and 86 points for their 2012 Cabernet Sauvignon Select Reserve. Frankly those ratings are what the late General Norman Schwarzkopf Jr. would refer to as "bovine scatology". I'd like to see them taste Markko under a blind-tasting forum against California and the rest and see what the ratings are then. There is too much bias amongst many of these so-called great tasters. The "Winestream Media", you know the wine snobs who think only their opinions matter, believe the masses should accept their words as gospel and blindly follow. That's a bunch of "bovine scatology" too. These wine snobs have anointed California as king, Oregon and Washington share the queen title, New York is made a bishop at best whereas Michigan and Virginia might be pawns. Where are Ohio and Pennsylvania? The answer is not on the radars of these elitist wine know-it-alls. As Dr. Frank told Arnie, you need recognition and without any coverage, it makes recognition almost impossible to earn.

The Final Verse: 50th Anniversary of Markko Vineyards (1968 – 2018) – Time to Celebrate

The final verse of the Gospel according to Arnie is simple. We need to celebrate 50 years of Markko Vineyard and Arnie Esterer, the region's true pioneer and the one who proved Dr. Frank's vision that vinifera grapes can grow and flourish in NE Ohio. At 87 years old, at the time of writing this book, Arnie knows he won't be here to see if the Lake Erie wine region, the one he helped build, finds its signature grape.

Arnie told me once "The industry is not where I thought it would be after 50 years but it is heading in the right direction. There are good things going on at St. Josephs, Harpersfield, Mapleridge, Laurello and M Cellars just to name a few. I see a bright future especially here in Conneaut. They will get there no matter what. They will discover themselves, but it won't happen too quickly. Leon Adams told me the process moves really slowly. Markko is a demonstration of what can be done in Ohio with vinifera wine making and growing wine grapes. Markko is a chapter in the long progression to follow."

Will Markko continue on after Arnie is gone? I believe it will. The vision of a family winery is what Arnie wanted from day one back in 1968. David, the second generation of the family, is talking with Arnie about taking the reins of the winery. Arnie is glad to hear that David is serious about stepping in sometime and, hopefully, it will happen sooner rather than later. We can only hope.

I remember one of Arnie's good friends, Dan Ross, doing a toast to Arnie. Dan's toast was "I've been coming out to Markko for 30 years and I feel we have the best Ohio winemaker right here. The guy, who founded Ohio State vinifera wines, puts magic in the bottle and still is the best winemaker...Arnie Esterer!" Arnie smiled and simply said "Thank you."

Arnie Esterer – Cheers!

Notes

1. Leon D. Adams *"The Wines of America"*, Second Edition, 1978, McGraw-Hill Book Company

2. Memo from Ohio Department of Agriculture, 12-Sep-2017 *"Ohio Grape and Wine Industry Contributes $1.3 Billion to State's Economy"*.

3. Philip R. Hines *"The Wines and Wineries of Ohio"*, copyright 1973, The Chronicle

4. Webster's Ninth New Collegiate Dictionary, 1989

5. Article *"Markko Vineyard – Ashtabula winemaker Arnie Esterer expands the possibilities of Ohio wine"*, by Steve Corso, Fall 2013, Edible Cleveland

6. Ohio Grape Industries Committee website; *www.findohiowines. com* (March 2018)

7. Miscellaneous Bulletin 111 *"Cultural Practices for Commercial Vineyards"*, New York State College of Agriculture and Life Sciences, A Statutory College of the State University, at Cornell University, December 1980.

8. Jacques Fanet *"Great Wine Terroirs"* University of California Press 2004 <u>ISBN</u> <u>0-520-23858-3</u>

9. Arnie Esterer *"The Gadding Vine"*, November 16, 2018 – Markko Vineyard

10. Kate Esterer *"The Gadding Vine"* No. 25, Fall 1990 – Markko Vineyard

11. Kate Esterer *"The Gadding Vine"*, No. 3, Fall 1978 – Markko Vineyard

12. Article in The New York Times *"Philip M. Wagner, 92, Wine Maker Who Introduced Hybrids"* by Frank J. Prial, January 3, 1997.

13. Philip M. Wagner *"A Wine-Growers Guide"* The Wine Appreciation Guild San Francisco, Third Edition January 1995.

14. André Tchelistcheff – *"André The Voice of Wine – The Story"*; http://themaestrofilm.com/thestory.htm

15. *"Complete Napa Valley California Wine History from Early 1800s to Today"*; http://www.thewinecellarinsider.com/california-wine/california-wine-history-from-early-plantings-in-1800s-to-today/

16. Kate Esterer *"The Gadding Vine"*, No. 12, Fall 1983 – Markko Vineyard

17. Arnie Esterer *"The Gadding Vine"*, No. 47, Summer 2000 – Markko Vineyards

18. *"Presque Isle Wine Cellars History"*; https://www.piwine.com/ourbusiness.html

19. *"The American Wine Society – A History of Sharing Wine Knowledge"*, American Wine Society website https://www.americanwinesociety.org/page/aboutus

20. Clifford Annis Interview notes from recordings of the session *"Dr. Konstantin's "Co-Operators" and Friends – Historic Tale/ Memories of Dr. Frank"*; American Wine Society (AWS) 50th Anniversary Conference, November 3, 2017, Pocono Manor, Pennyslvania

21. Christopher Johnston *"Allen C. Holmes, Activist for Community Enhancement, 1920–1990: 1987 Special Citation for Distinguished Service to the Art"* – courtesy of http://cleveland-artsprize.org/awardees/allen_holmes.html

22. Howard G. Goldberg *"Leon Adams, Wine Expert And Writer, 90"* – courtesy of https://www.nytimes.com/1995/09/16/obituaries/leon-adams-wine-expert-and-writer-90.html

23. Joseph Cooper Obituary – courtesy of http://www.legacy.com/obituaries/dispatch/obituary.aspx?n=joseph-cooper&pid=143430703&fhid=8657

24. Letter from Dr. Konstantin Frank to Arnie Esterer, December 15, 1970.

25. Randy Ullom profile, Kendall-Jackson website, http://www.kj.com/people/randy-ullom

26. Dr. Roland Riesen profile, https://www.changins.ch/professors.html

27. *"Ken's Wine Guide"*, definition of Sur lie, https://www.kenswineguide.com/wine.php?word=66

28. The Maisonette Restaurant, https://en.wikipedia.org/wiki/The_Maisonette

29. Peggy Kirk Hall *"Ohio Creates New "Farm Winery" Liquor Permit"*https://farmoffice.osu.edu/blog-tags/ohio-farm-winery-liquor-permit, July 7, 2016

30. *"Ohio Wine Hall of Fame"*, https://www.ohiowines.org/label/

31. *"The Cork Report"*, http://thecorkreport.us/about-the-cork-report/

32. Tom Russ *"Finger Lakes Wines and the Legacy of Dr. Konstantin Frank"*, first edition, 2015, American Palate, A Division of the The History Press

Index

Italicized page numbers indicate photographs.

Fournier, Charles, 61
France, winemaking in, 7, 29, 78, 85, 105, 108
Frank, Konstantin (Dr. Frank)
    American Wine Society and, 59–61
    as Arnie's teacher, 22–27, 72, 76
    Homage Chardonnay for, 93, *94*
    on hybrid grapes, 27, 61, 72, 90
    influence of, 3, 60–61, 108
    Markko Vineyards, visit to, 87
    Petry, Brother David and, 62
    photograph of, *22*
    on vinifera grapes, 72–73, 81, 93, 104, 106
    Wagner (Philip) and, 28
Frisbie, Chris, 47
Frisbie, Denis, 37, 47–48, 75
Frisbie, Linda
    Cabernet wines and, 88, 105
    death of son, 47–48
    funny stories, 65, 99, 102
    Hubbard (Tim) and, 42–43
    impact on vineyard, 2, 30–31, 46–48, 50–51
    love of family, 49
    memorial poem for, 52–54
    Mingot (Hélène) and, 78–79
    photographs of, *37, 45*
    on tasting groups, 100–101
    wine palate of, 47, 50–51, 78–79, 91, 107
Funny stories, 33–35, 98–102

G
The Gadding Vine (newsletter), 6, 14–15, 37, 43
Gallander, James F., 81
Gerlosky, Wes, 76
Gharsallah-Nuernberg, Ali, 96

I

International Paper, 10–11
International Wine and Food Society, 55, 65, 67, 71

J

Jackson, Jess, 79
Jarvey, Chris, 36
Jeff (crew), 37
Jennifer (crew), 101
Johns, Greg
    on Esterer (Arnie), 74–76, 82–83, 95, 101
    on Frisbie (Linda), 49–51
    on future of Markko Vineyards, 75–76
    on Markko crew, 30
    photograph of, *82*
    on Riesen (Roland), 80
    on tasting groups, 100–101
Johnson Estates, 79
Johnston, Christopher, 65
Jordan, T.D., 5

K

Kelly, Lucilla, 31, 36, 37
Kendall-Jackson Winery, 78, 79
Kids at winery, 17, 98–99
Kmiecik, Tom and Joyce, 48
Konnerth, Bill, 20, 55–58, 59

L

Lake Erie Appellation. *See also* Terroir
    native grapes in, 3–4
    Pinot Gris as signature grape in, 24–27, 91–93, 105–106
    potential of, 8, 106–110
    vinifera grapes in, 2–3, 4–8, 90–91, 103–110

Acknowledgements

Every writer who takes on the task of writing a book requires the assistance of many to make the dream of the book become a reality. Writing the story of Arnie Esterer and Markko Vineyard could not have been accomplished without the help from family, friends, colleagues and just plain fans of Markko. Tom Russ said it best in the acknowledgement he wrote for his book *Finger Lakes Wines and the Legacy of Dr. Konstantin Frank*, "The challenge of acknowledging those who have helped is trying to include everyone."[32] I will do my best not to leave anyone out but accept my apologies right now if I miss you.

First off, the biggest thank you goes to Arnulf Esterer for agreeing to allow a first time author to tell his story. Arnie graciously allowed me to become part of the Markko wine family over four years. Arnie spent many hours answering questions, going through files that contain some of the history of Markko and provided contacts for people I should talk to. Most importantly I thank him for allowing me to pick his memory about Linda Frisbie, Tim Hubbard, Joe Cooper, Leon Adams, Brother David Petry and Allen Holmes, all who have left this world. Their contributions to Markko never left Arnie's memory or heart. Thank you, Arnie, for your friendship.

A big thank you to Greg Johns, whose longtime friendship with Arnie provided insights on him, Linda and the Markko family that only someone close to Arnie could provide. I appreciate your humor throughout this process.

Doug Moorhead provided some revelations on Dr. Frank at the 2017 American Wine Society tribute and I'm thankful I was able to attend. Though my planned interview with Doug Moorhead never happened due to his stroke, Marlene Moorhead provided insights on Doug that were invaluable and I'm grateful to her and wish Doug only the best and a speedy recovery.

I want to acknowledge the legion of Markko friends I spoke with during the research for the book. I can't list them all but want to specifically thank Tom and Joyce Kmiecik, Dan Ross, Bill Ross, John "JP" Piero, Mario Guarraccino, Ron DePascale, Bruce Robishaw, Martta Tuomaala, and Jerry Danacheck for providing their memories of Arnie and Markko Vineyard.

David Esterer was kind enough to spend a few hours with me to talk about his Dad, Mom, and his memories of growing up at Markko Vineyard and I'm grateful to him for that. I want to acknowledge the contributions of Culette Burdette, Ted Burdette, Nancy Allen, Christopher "Swabby" Jarvi and the entire Markko Crew for making me feel like a part of the family and making me laugh every day I visited Markko.

I'd especially like to thank Frederick Frank, grandson of Dr. Konstantin Frank, of Dr. Frank Wines for graciously writing the foreword for the book and providing encouragement to tell Arnie's story.

Every writer needs a mentor and mine is Thomas Pellechia. I want to thank Thomas for spending time with me early on because it was that meeting at the Village Tavern in Hammondsport, New York that convinced me I could write Arnie's story. I was originally contemplating a book about Ohio winemakers and growers in general, but Thomas was the one who suggested the book be about Arnie and Markko Vineyard. Thomas is a great writer and I only wish I could be considered his student. Again, thank you Thomas!

Jeff and Sheila Stockert were critical in providing a sounding board on this self-publishing journey. In addition, many thanks to John Burns for donating his time and using his artistic magic and genius to create the posters used at the book signings. Thank you my friends. I would like to thank Jim Messenheimer for taking some of the pictures that appear in the book. I especially thank him for the front and back covers.

I want to thank all my wine friends who taste every Saturday and Sunday at Buehler's in Jackson Township, Ohio and encouraged me from day one. I will try to name them all but I will surely miss a few: Judy and Gary Connor, John Burns, Jeff and Sheila Stockert, Doris Lonas, Gail Terner Borowski, Gwen Aquino, Julie Riley, Sandra Taylor, Jim and Tricia Marks, John and Lorraine Kessler, Sandy Miller, Jeff Oyster, Patricia Robinson, John Allensworth, Ken and Trish May, Trish O'Connor, Ashlie Lyn Fabiny, Keri Dressel Hoffer, Emily Gareis, Robin Schumacher, Conni Babcock and Roger Diehl.

My book would not have been possible without the crack editing of my better half Dana Annis, my wife of 30 plus years, whose sharp critique was indispensable. Thank you my dear, you have my love and gratitude always!

If there are any errors in the book, I take full responsibility for that. There was quite a bit of information left out and I had to make the decision on what to use and what not to. That was the challenge. My goal was to tell the story of Arnie and Markko Vineyard guided by Arnie's memory and words.

About the Author

Clifford (Cliff) Annis, Jr. is a Senior Consultant at PAREXEL Consulting and this is his first book. He grew-up in the Finger Lakes region, spending parts of his summers throughout middle and high school at the cottage of his great-aunt on Keuka Lake. He travels all over the world for his work and tasting wines from different regions he visits is one of his passions and pleasures. He and his wife, Dana, have two grown children, Megan and Matthew, who are both starting to appreciate "the fruits of the vines".